Correct by Design with TLA+
Early Preview

Richard Tang

February 24, 2025

Acknowledgement

A big thanks to Anthony Giardina for reviewing the content of this book.

Contents

III   Examples with PlusCal   85

IV   System Modeling   99

Part I

Introduction

Chapter 1

Motivation

1.1 Catching Problems Early

Years ago, I worked on a proprietary low-power processor in an embedded system. The processor ran a microcode featuring a custom instruction set. To enter a low-power state, a set (possibly hundreds) of instructions were executed. These instructions progressively put the system in a lower power state. For example: Turn off IP A, then turn off IP B, then turn off the power island to the IPs. To save cost and power, the low-power processor had very limited debuggability support.

An experienced reader may start to notice some red flags.

If the microcode attempts to access the memory interface when the power island has been shut off, the processor will hang. Since the debug power island has been shut off, the physical hardware debug port is also unavailable, leaving the developer with *no way* of live debugging problems. At this point, the developer needs to search through numerous instructions to catch system constraint violations (invariants) *manually*.

As one can imagine, maintaining the microcode was very expensive. Fortunately, the proprietary low-power processor only had a handful

of instructions, so I created a simulator for this proprietary processor
to verify the microcode before deploying it on-target. The simulator
models the processor states as a state graph, with executed instruction,
transitions the state machine to the next state. At every state, all the
invariants are verified. Example invariants include:

- Accessing memory interface after power off leads to a hang

- Accessing certain register in certain chip revision leads to a hang

- Verify IPs are shut off in the allowed order

The verification algorithm was implemented using a *depth-first-search*,
providing 100% microcode coverage before deployment on target.

In reality, any system can be modeled as an arbitrary set of states
with a collection of invariants that be true at all times. The complexity of such an arbitrary system generally grows quadratically as
the number of states grows linearly (eg. in an N-state system, adding
state N+1 may introduce N transitions into the new state). Many
engineering problems have a large number of states, such as lockless
or wait-free data structures, distributed algorithms, OS schedulers,
consensus protocols, and more. As the number of states grows, the
problem becomes more challenging for designers to reason about.

So, how do we produce a system that is *correct by design?*

1.2   The Generalized Problem

Fast forward to now: I stumbled across TLA+, a formalized solution
of what I was looking for.

In the age of big data, vertical scaling is no longer sufficient. The
industry has been exploring and implementing horizontal scaling so-
lutions for past two decades. Instead of focusing on increasing clock
speed, hardwares vendor has been focusing on adding more instances
of hardware in their design. On the other hand, software vendors
has been designing horizontal scaling solution that takes advantage of
large volume of commodity hardware. There is one small problem.

Horizontal scaling requires concurrent reasoning, and:

Humans are not good at concurrent reasoning.

Our cognitive system is optimized for sequential reasoning. Enumerating all scenarios in one's mind to ensure an arbitrary design accommodates all the corner cases is challenging.

Consider a distributed system. The system is a cluster of independently operating entities, which collectively needs to offer the correct system behavior. At any given time, nodes in the cluster may crash, restart, receive instructions out-of-order, etc.

Consider a single producer multiple consumer lockless queue. The consumers may reserve an index in the queue in a certain order but may release it in a different order. What if one reader is slow, and another reader is superfast and possibly lapses the slow reader?

Consider an OS scheduler with locks. Assume all the processes have the same priority. Can a process starve the other processes by repeatedly acquiring and releasing the lock? How do we ensure scheduling is fair?

The *anti-pattern* is to band-aid the design until the bugs stop coming. This is never ideal, and a hard-to-reproduce crashing bug will come in at the most inconvenient time. How do we make sure the system is *correct by design*? To solve this problem, we must rely on tools to do the reasoning *for us*.

1.3   What is TLA+?

TLA+ is a *system specification language*, allowing the designer to describe a system as a set of states with transitions. Designers can describe safety properties that must hold in every state, and liveness properties that must hold for a sequence of states.

Once the system is modeled as a set of states, the states can be *exhaustively* explored (via breath-first-search) to ensure properties are upheld throughout the entire state space (either per state or a sequence of states).

When designing a system, designer tend to focus on the obvious happy and unhappy path, and create corresponding tests to provide coverage. Unless the system is trivial, designers often miss subtle cases that can cause violations. These tend to be caught during verification, at which points more tests are added to prevent future escapes.

The *superpower* of TLA+ is it will exhaustively cover *all* states and transitions before the design even enters verification. Consider the following example system state graph:

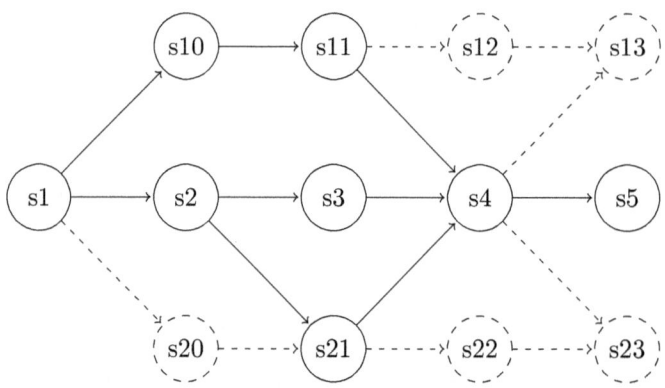

The solid states and edges are the ones designer has accounted for, and the rest are state and transition the designer missed. A large part of the missed states and transitions may be inconsequential, but a subset of these may be catastrophic failure states that require explicit handling or re-architecting.

The best way to look at TLA+ is it is a *thinking tool*. Once the designer specifies the system with allowed transitions and safety properties, the model checker will identify cases where violations can occur and the set of transitions that led up to the violations.

Amazon AWS has used TLA+ to identify a bug that occurs after 35 transitions [14]. As humans, we are reasonably good at describing the *top-level* design, but need a tool like TLA+ to identify all the *dark corners* of the design.

1.4 About This Book

The book intends to teach the reader how to write TLA+ specification for their design to provide confidence in its *correctness*. This book is targeted to software designers, hardware designers, system architects, and in general anyone interested in designing correct systems.

To get the most out of the book, the reader is expected to have general computer science knowledge. The reader doesn't need to be an expert in a particular language to understand this book; TLA+ is effectively its own language. This book is example-driven and will go through designs such as lockless queues, simple task schedulers, consensus algorithms, etc. Readers will likely enjoy a deeper insight if there is familiarity with these topics.

1.5 How to Use This Book

This book was designed to be used as a reference, providing examples and references using TLA+.

This book is split into multiple parts, covering TLA+ native notation, PlusCal (C-like syntax that transpiles down to TLA+ native notation), and rapid prototyping with TLA+. All examples will follow a similar layout, covering the problem statement, design, specification, safety and liveness properties.

All examples in this book will be presented using TLA+ *mathematical notation*. Converting between Mathematical and ASCII notation is assumed trivial due to the one-to-one mapping. Readers are encouraged to consult Table 8 in [1] as needed.

The last part of the book provides language references and focused discussion on various topics such as liveness, fairness, patterns, etc.

Chapter 2

TLA+ Primer

2.1 Purpose

The key insight to TLA+ is modeling a system as a state machine. A simple digital clock can be represented by two variables: hour and minute. The number of possible states in a digital clock is $24 * 60 = 1440$. For example, a clock in state 10:00 will transition to state 10:01. Assume an arbitrary system described by N variables, each variable having K possible values. Such an arbitrary system can have up to N^K states.

For every specification, the designer can specify *safety* properties (or invariants) that must be true in *every* state. For example, in any state of the digital clock, hour *must* be between 0 to 23, or formally described as *hour* $\in 0..23$. Similarly, the minute must have a value between 0 to 59, or *minute* $\in 0..59$. Examples of invariants of a system include: Only one thread has exclusive access to a critical region, all variables in the system are within allowable value, and the resource allocation manager never allocates more than available resources.

The designer can also specify *liveness* properties. These are properties to be satisfied by a *sequence of states*. One liveness property of the digital clock could be when the clock is 10:00, it will eventually become 11:00 (10:00 *leads* to 11:00). Example liveness property include:

a distributed system eventually converges, the scheduler eventually schedules every task in the task queue, and the resource allocation manager fairly allocates resources.

A TLA+ specification can be checked by TLC, the model checker. TLC uses *breadth-first search* algorithm to explore *all* states in the state machine and ensure safety and liveness properties are upheld.

A TLA+ specification describes the system using *temporal logic*. The syntax may appear unfamiliar due to its syntax. Just like learning any other programming language, an enthusiastic reader can become familiarized fairly quickly.

2.2   Design

In this example, we will specify a *digital clock*. The digital clock has a few simple requirements:

- Two variables to represent state: hour and minute

- The clock increments one minute at a time

- Hour is between 0 to 23, inclusive

- Minute is between 0 to 59, inclusive

- Clock wraps around at midnight (ie. 23:59 transitions to 00:00)

The state graph for the clock looks like this:

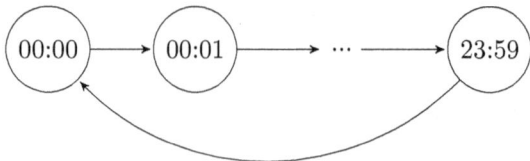

Note that in this particular example each state only has one entry and one exit. TLA+ doesn't preclude states with multiple entries and multiple exists.

2.3 Spec

The *Init* state of such a system can be described as:

$Init \triangleq$
  $\wedge\ hour = 0$
  $\wedge\ minute = 0$

$\triangleq$ is the *defines equal* symbol and $\wedge$ is the *logical and* symbol. The above TLA+ syntax can be read as *Init* state is defined as both hour and minute are 0.

The specification also always includes a *Next* definition, an *action formula* describing how the system transitions from one state to another. Action formula contains *primed* variables, representing values of variables in their next state. The *Next* action for the digital clock can be defined as:

$NextHour \triangleq$
  $\wedge\ minute = 59$
  $\wedge\ hour' = (hour + 1)\%24$
  $\wedge\ minute' = 0$
$NextMinute \triangleq$
  $\wedge\ minute \neq 59$
  $\wedge\ hour' = hour$
  $\wedge\ minute' = minute + 1$
$Next \triangleq$
  $\vee\ NextMinute$
  $\vee\ NextHour$

Here's a breakdown of what the specification does:

- *Next* can take either *NextHour* or *NextMinute*. $\vee$ is the *logical or* operator.

- *Next* takes *NextMinute* when *minute* is not 59. When *NextMinute* takes: *hour* in the next state equals to *hour* in the current state, but *minute* in the next state is *minute* in current state plus one.

- *Next* takes *NextHour* when *minute* is 59. When *NextMinute* takes: *hour* in the next state equals to *hour* in the current state plus one and modulus by number of hours in a day and *minute* in the next state equals to zero.

Note that the formulas are *state descriptions*, not *assignment*. *minute = 59* describes the state transition takes when minute *equals* 59. Since this is an equality description, *minute = 59* and *59 = minute* are equivalent in TLA+.

Finally, the *Spec* itself is formally defined as:

$$
\begin{aligned}
vars &\triangleq \langle hour,\ minute \rangle \\
Spec &\triangleq \\
&\land Init \\
&\land \Box[Next]_{vars}
\end{aligned}
$$

Note this forms the basis for **all** TLA+ specification. Every example in this book will include a *Spec* definition similar to this.

$\Box[Next]_{vars}$ deserves some special attention:

- *vars* is defined earlier to be *all* variables in the specification, in this case, hour and minute. A combination of these variables at different values constitutes the states of the system (eg. 23:59 and 00:00 are different states in the system).

- $\Box[Next]_{vars}$ is a box-action formula, where *Next* is an action and *vars* is a state function.

- $\Box$ (necessity operator) asserts the formula is always true for every step in the behavior.

- Steps in the behaviour are defined as $[Next]_{vars}$, where *Next* describes the action and *vars* capturing all variables representing the state.

This can be roughly translated to: the system is valid for every step *Next* can take.

2.4 Safety

A safety property describes an invariant that must hold in *every* state of the system. A common invariant is *type safety* checks. In a digital clock, an hour can only be in value between 0 to 23, and a minute can only be the value of 0 to 59:

$Type\_OK \triangleq$
$\quad \wedge hour \in 0 .. 23$
$\quad \wedge minute \in 0 .. 59$

When an hour or minute falls outside of the specified range, the model checker reports violation.

2.5 Liveness and Fairness

Liveness property verifies certain behaviors across a sequence of states. One liveness property is to confirm the clock wraps around at midnight, a property that can only be verified after checking at least two states:

$Liveness \triangleq$
$\quad \wedge hour = 23 \wedge minute = 59 \rightsquigarrow hour = 0 \wedge minute = 0$

$\rightsquigarrow$ is the *leads to* operator, suggesting something is eventually true. TLA+ provides a set of operators to describe the liveness property.

To verify liveness, we need to modify the specification slightly to enable *fairness* to prevent *stuttering*. In plain terms, fairness ensures a state always transitions to *some other state*. Without fairness, the specification is allowed to *stutter*, or *not transition* to any state. This fails the liveness property check as the model checker cannot verify the behavior across a sequence of states. To get a more comprehensive description of fairness, refer to the last part of the book.

$Spec \triangleq$
$\quad \wedge Init$

$$\wedge \Box[Next]_{vars}$$
$$\wedge \mathrm{WF}_{vars}(Next)$$

$WF_{vars}(Next)$ is the fairness qualifier.

2.6   Model Checker

A TLA+ specification can be verified using a model checker. The model checker runs the specification and verifies all specified safety and liveness properties are fulfilled. The model checker is a library written in Java and can be invoked from the command line. For instructions on installing the model checker and related tools, please see [3].

After installing the model checker, we need two things to verify the specification:

- clock.tla: specification

- clock.cfg: configuration

For reference, clock.tla is listed below:

```
─────────────────────── MODULE clock ───────────────────────
EXTENDS Naturals
VARIABLES hour, minute
vars ≜ ⟨hour, minute⟩
Type_OK ≜
        ∧ hour ∈ 0 .. 23
        ∧ minute ∈ 0 .. 59
Liveness ≜
        ∧ hour = 23 ∧ minute = 59 ↝ hour = 0 ∧ minute = 0
Init ≜
        ∧ hour = 0
        ∧ minute = 0
NextMinute ≜
        ∧ minute = 59
        ∧ hour' = (hour + 1)%24
```

$$\land\ minute' = 0$$
$$NextHour\ \triangleq$$
$$\quad \land\ minute \neq 59$$
$$\quad \land\ hour' = hour$$
$$\quad \land\ minute' = minute + 1$$
$$Next\ \triangleq$$
$$\quad \lor\ NextMinute$$
$$\quad \lor\ NextHour$$
$$Spec\ \triangleq$$
$$\quad \land\ Init$$
$$\quad \land\ \Box[Next]_{vars}$$
$$\quad \land\ \mathrm{WF}_{vars}(Next)$$

The corresponding clock.cfg is listed below:

```
SPECIFICATION Spec
INVARIANTS Type_OK
PROPERTIES Liveness
```

After putting both clock.cfg and clock.tla in the same directory, one can now run the model checker. In this book I'll assume a command line interface for the model checker:

```
java -cp /usr/local/lib/tla2tools.jar tlc2.TLC clock
...
Model checking completed. No error has been found.
...
The depth of the complete state graph search is 1440.
```

The 1440 states in the state graph represent the total number of minutes in a day.

Part II

Examples with TLA+

TLA+ notation is rooted in temporal logic and doesn't share the usual programming language *look and feel*. Despite the possibly foreign look, the core language semantics for TLA+ is reasonably constrained. This allows anyone with some programming experience to pick up relatively quickly. This section provides a collection of example TLA+ specification with increasing complexity, easing the readers into this wonderful tool.

Chapter 3

Dining Philosophers

Dining philosophers is a famous problem used to illustrate concurrent algorithm design [11]. The problem states there are N philosophers sitting in a circle, with a fork placed between each philosopher. This is illustrated below:

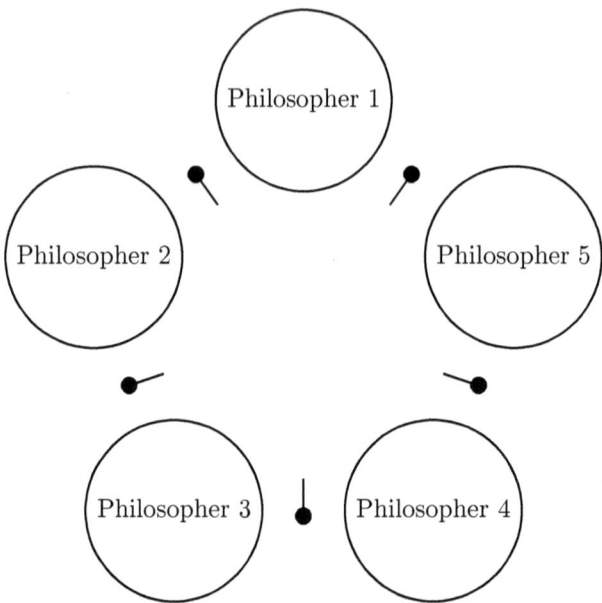

Each philosopher is either thinking or eating, but the philosopher needs to take *both* forks to eat. The problem is to design a solution that ensures one or more philosophers can eat when they want to.

A possible failing scenario is when *all* philosophers take the fork to their left. Now every philosopher is stuck waiting for the fork to their right, and every philosopher starve.

3.1 Design

Every philosopher behaves similarly:

- Take one fork
- Take another fork
- Eat
- Put away one fork
- Put away another fork

3.2 Spec

The core part of *Spec* looks like this:

$Next \triangleq$
 $\lor \exists\, k \in 0 \ldots P - 1:$
 TakeFirst(k)
 $\lor \exists\, k \in 0 \ldots P - 1:$
 TakeSecond(k)
 $\lor \exists\, k \in 0 \ldots P - 1:$
 Eat(k)
 $\lor \exists\, k \in 0 \ldots P - 1:$
 PutFirst(k)
 $\lor \exists\, k \in 0 \ldots P - 1:$
 PutSecond(k)

This reflects the behavior described earlier. Note that there's a sequential dependency to these actions. The philosopher can only take the second fork after taking the first fork, eat after having both forks and put away the forks after eating.

$First(k) \triangleq k$
$Second(k) \triangleq (k + 1)\%P$

$TakeFirst(k) \triangleq$
 $\land\; eaten[k] = 0$
 $\land\; forks[First(k)] = UNUSED$
 $\land\; \text{UNCHANGED } eaten$

$TakeSecond(k) \triangleq$
 $\land\; eaten[k] = 0$
 $\land\; forks[First(k)] = k$
 $\land\; forks[Second(k)] = UNUSED$
 $\land\; forks' = [forks \text{ EXCEPT } ![Second(k)] = k]$
 $\land\; \text{UNCHANGED } eaten$

The philosopher greedily takes the first fork when possible. After the philosopher has the first fork, she greedily takes the second fork when possible.

$Eat(k) \triangleq$
LET
$\quad$ $left \triangleq k$
$\quad$ $right \triangleq (k+1)\%P$
IN
$\quad$ $\wedge forks[left] = k$
$\quad$ $\wedge forks[right] = k$
$\quad$ $\wedge eaten' = [eaten \text{ EXCEPT } ![k] = 1]$
$\quad$ $\wedge$ UNCHANGED $forks$

Once the philosopher has both forks, she can eat.

$PutFirst(k) \triangleq$
$\quad$ $\wedge eaten[k] = 1$
$\quad$ $\wedge forks[First(k)] = k$
$\quad$ $\wedge forks' = [forks \text{ EXCEPT } ![First(k)] = UNUSED]$
$\quad$ $\wedge$ UNCHANGED $eaten$

$PutSecond(k) \triangleq$
$\quad$ $\wedge eaten[k] = 1$
$\quad$ $\wedge forks[First(k)] \neq k$
$\quad$ $\wedge forks[Second(k)] = k$
$\quad$ $\wedge forks' = [forks \text{ EXCEPT } ![Second(k)] = UNUSED]$
$\quad$ $\wedge eaten' = [eaten \text{ EXCEPT } ![k] = 0]$

After eating, the philosopher puts away the forks.

3.3   Safety

Omitted for this chapter.

3.4   Liveness

One liveness property is to ensure that at least one philosopher can eat when she wants to under all circumstances:

$Liveness \triangleq$
  $\exists\, k \in 0\,..\,P-1:$
    $\wedge\ eaten[k] = 0 \rightsquigarrow eaten[k] = 1$
    $\wedge\ eaten[k] = 1 \rightsquigarrow eaten[k] = 0$

However, *Spec* defined as is doesn't implement any deadlock mitigation. Running it against the model the checker results in the following violations:

```
State 2: <TakeFirst line 19, col 5 to line 23,
    col 22 of module dining>
/\ eaten = (0 :> 0 @@ 1 :> 0 @@ 2 :> 0)
/\ forks = (0 :> 0 @@ 1 :> 100 @@ 2 :> 100)

State 3: <TakeFirst line 19, col 5 to line 23,
    col 22 of module dining>
/\ eaten = (0 :> 0 @@ 1 :> 0 @@ 2 :> 0)
/\ forks = (0 :> 0 @@ 1 :> 1 @@ 2 :> 100)

State 4: <TakeFirst line 19, col 5 to line 23,
    col 22 of module dining>
/\ eaten = (0 :> 0 @@ 1 :> 0 @@ 2 :> 0)
/\ forks = (0 :> 0 @@ 1 :> 1 @@ 2 :> 2)
```

When all philosopher takes their left fork, no one can eat.

A simple fix to the problem is for every philosopher to take the fork with the smaller index first:

$First(k) \triangleq$ IF $k \neq P-1$ THEN k ELSE 0
$Second(k) \triangleq$ IF $k \neq P-1$ THEN $k+1$ ELSE k

When the philosopher with the highest index wants to eat, she will need to take fork 0 first. In the case where all other philosophers have already taken their first fork, the philosopher with the highest index will fail to take her first fork (because it has already been taken by the first philosopher). This allows the philosopher with the second-highest index to make progress, thus preventing a deadlock.

The model checker will pass the updated *Spec*.

Chapter 4

Strongly Connected Components

In a graph, a strongly connected component (SCC) is a subset of vertices where every pair of vertices are reachable from each other. An example graph with four SCCs is illustrated below, where the vertices that share the same color and belong in the same SCC:

A node is an SCC by itself. There are many applications of SCCs, including: social network analysis, web crawling, and software modularity analysis.

TLA+ also uses SCCs to verify the liveness properties of a specification. Consider the following graph from a hypothetical specification:

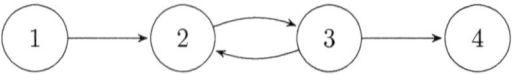

States 2 and 3 form an SCC. Assume the system has a liveness property that defines state 1 *leads to* state 4. The model checker can fail the specification because execution may be trapped inside the SSC (unless a fairness description is provided). The model checker must first identify all SCCs in the graph to verify liveness. This explains why verifying liveness non-trivially increases model checker runtime, because the SCC identifying algorithm implemented in the model checker runs linearly.

In this chapter, we will implement a horizontally scalable SCC detection algorithm described in *A GPU Algorithm for Detecting Strongly Connected Components* [12].

4.1   Design

The following provides the pseudocode description of the parallel SCC detection algorithm as described in the paper:

1: *converged* ← *false*
2: **while** not *converged* **do**
    ▷ Initialize vertex
3:    **for all** vertices $v \in V$ **do**
4:       $v_{in} \leftarrow v_{id}$
5:       $v_{out} \leftarrow v_{id}$
6:    **end for**
    ▷ Propagate max value
7:    *updated* ← *false*
8:    **while** *updated* **do**
9:       **for all** edges $(u-> v) \in E$ **do**
10:         $v_{out} \leftarrow max(u_{out}, v_{out})$
11:         $v_{in} \leftarrow max(u_{in}, v_{in})$
12:       **end for**
13:       *updated* ← at least one v_{in} or v_{out} value changed
14:    **end while**

15:        ▷ Remove edges that span SCC
15:        **for all** edges $(u \rightarrow v) \in E$ **do**
16:              **if** $u_{in} \neq v_{in}$ or $u_{out} \neq v_{out}$ **then**
17:                    $E \leftarrow E\ (u \rightarrow v)$
18:              **end if**
19:        **end for**
20: **end while**

The algorithm is split into three parts: initialization, max value propagation and edge trimming.

4.2   Specification

Spec is defined into three phases: *Init*, *Update*, *Trim*. Phase *Init* is defined as follow:

$PhaseInit \triangleq$

$\quad \wedge phase =$ "Init"

$\quad \wedge phase' =$ "Update"

$\quad \wedge edges' = new\_edges$

$\quad \wedge new\_edges' = new\_edges$

$\quad \wedge in' = [k \in Vertex \mapsto k]$

$\quad \wedge out' = [k \in Vertex \mapsto k]$

$\quad \wedge updated' = 0$

$\quad \wedge converged' = 0$

in and *out* are defined as lookup table using *functions*.

The *Update* phase implements max value propagation:

$PhaseUpdate \triangleq$

$\wedge\ phase =$ "Update"

$\wedge\ \vee\ \wedge\ \exists\, e \in edges :$

  LET

$$src \triangleq e[1]$$
$$dst \triangleq e[2]$$

  IN

$\wedge\ in' = [in\ \text{EXCEPT}\ ![dst] = Max(in[src],\ in[dst])]$

$\wedge\ out' = [out\ \text{EXCEPT}\ ![src] = Max(out[src],\ out[dst])]$

$\wedge\ edges' = edges \setminus \{e\}$

$\wedge\ \vee\ \wedge\ in' \neq in\ \vee\ out' \neq out$

$\wedge\ updated' = 1$

$\vee\ \wedge\ in' = in\ \wedge\ out' = out$

$\wedge\ updated' = 0$

$\wedge\ \text{UNCHANGED}\ \langle new\_edges,\ phase,\ converged \rangle$

$\vee\ \wedge\ edges = \{\}$

$\wedge\ updated = 0$

$\wedge\ phase' =$ "Trim"

$\wedge\ \text{UNCHANGED}\ \langle edges,\ new\_edges,\ in,\ out,\ updated,\ converged \rangle$

$\vee\ \wedge\ edges = \{\}$

$\wedge\ updated \neq 0$

$\wedge\ edges' = new\_edges$

$\wedge\ \text{UNCHANGED}\ \langle phase,\ new\_edges,\ in,\ out,\ updated,\ converged \rangle$

The edge iteration loop is implemented with an existential qualifier over edges. After processing an edge, the edge is removed from the set edges to simulate so it is not chosen again in the next iteration. Once set edges become empty, the algorithm determines if we need to repeat the propagation process.

The following implements phase *trim*:

$Phase\,Trim \;\triangleq$

    $\wedge\; phase = \text{``Trim''}$

    $\wedge\; \vee\; \wedge\; edges = \{\}$

    $\wedge\; in = out$

    $\wedge\; converged' = 1$

    $\wedge\; \text{UNCHANGED } \langle phase,\ new\_edges,\ edges,\ in,\ out,\ updated \rangle$

    $\vee\; \wedge\; edges = \{\}$

    $\wedge\; in \neq out$

    $\wedge\; phase' = \text{``Init''}$

    $\wedge\; \text{UNCHANGED } \langle in,\ new\_edges,\ edges,\ out,\ updated,\ converged \rangle$

    $\vee\; \wedge\; edges \neq \{\}$

    $\wedge\; \exists\, e \in edges :$

      LET

          $src \;\triangleq\; e[1]$

          $dst \;\triangleq\; e[2]$

      IN

          $\wedge\; \vee\; \wedge\; out[src] \neq out[dst] \vee in[src] \neq in[dst]$

          $\wedge\; new\_edges' = new\_edges \setminus \{e\}$

          $\vee\; \wedge\; out[src] = out[dst] \wedge in[src] = in[dst]$

          $\wedge\; \text{UNCHANGED } new\_edges$

          $\wedge\; edges' = edges \setminus \{e\}$

    $\wedge\; \text{UNCHANGED } \langle phase,\ in,\ out,\ updated,\ converged \rangle$

Similar to the previous phase, we use existential qualifiers and set subtraction to simulate iterating through all edges. Another variable *new_edges* is used to track edges to be used in the next iteration if required.

4.3   Safety

To find the solution of a given graph, let us define a safety property where converged is always 0:

$Termination \;\triangleq$

    $converged = 0$

In other words, we want the model checker to terminate when converged becomes 1.

Let us assume input similar to as defined in the paper:

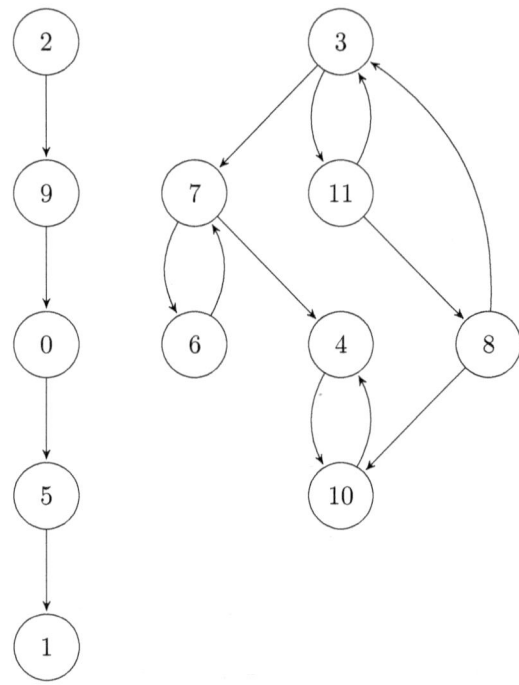

Running the model checker against the specification outputs the following:

```
Error: Invariant Termination is violated.
Error: The behavior up to this point is:
...
State 15: <PhaseTrim line 76, col 5 to line 96,
    col 61 of module scc>
/\ out = ( 0 :> 0 @@
    1 :> 1 @@
    2 :> 2 @@
```

```
 3 :> 11 @@
 4 :> 10 @@
 5 :> 5 @@
 6 :> 7 @@
 7 :> 7 @@
 8 :> 11 @@
 9 :> 9 @@
10 :> 10 @@
11 :> 11 )
...
```

As defined by the algorithm, vertices sharing the same value are part of the same SCC. The specification correctly identifies three SCCs with more than one vertex: {3, 8, 11}, {6, 7} and {4, 10}.

4.4 Liveness

Omitted for this chapter.

Chapter 5

Simple Scheduler

Task schedulers are ubiquitous. Every device implements *something* to manage tasks. Modern desktop or mobile device processes are nontrivial OS abstractions. Every process maintains its own virtual memory space, and the context-switching process requires the OS to "clean" the hardware before running the new process for security reasons.

For embedded devices such as hard drives or network cards, the security consideration may be relaxed as users are typically not allowed to run arbitrary code on the device. Sometimes these products don't have a full-blown operating system to save on memory and storage footprint but still need some scheduler to manage the tasks.

To solve the C10k [10] problem, languages like Rust supports asynchronous programming. Asynchronous programming enables task scheduling *within* a process to scale up system throughput. However, Rust only provides *language support* for asynchronous programming, and user must supply their runtime. The runtime must also include a scheduler to manage the tasks inside the process.

In this chapter, we will implement a very simple cooperative scheduler with tasks that share a single lock.

5.1   Design

The task scheduler has the following features:

- Supporting N execution context (ie. CPUs).

- Supporting T number of tasks.

- Tasks have identical priorities and are scheduled cooperatively.

- System shares a single locked resource.

- Any task can attempt to access the resource. Any task attempting to access the resource is guaranteed to have access at some point.

- If multiple tasks attempt to access the lock, the tasks will be scheduled in lock request order.

5.2   Specification

We will model the scheduler using the following variables:

$Init \triangleq$
$\quad \land cpus = [i \in 0 .. N - 1 \mapsto \text{""}]$
$\quad \land ready\_q = SetToSeq(Tasks)$
$\quad \land blocked\_q = \langle \rangle$
$\quad \land lock\_owner = \text{""}$

A few things to note:

- The system has N executing context, represented as number of CPUs. When a task is running, $cpus[k]$ is set to $taskName$. When the CPU is idle, $tcpus[k]$ is set to an empty string.

- $ready\_q$ and $blocked\_q$ are initialized as *ordered tuple*, due to the cooperative scheduling requirement.

- $SetToSeq$ is a macro from the community module [4] to convert a set into an ordered tuple. To use the community module, one can install required .tla files into the TLA+ project source directly.

- *lock_owner* represents the task that is currently holding the lock.

A task can be in three possible states: *Ready, Blocked,* and *Running.* The Spec describes required lock contention handling.

$Ready \triangleq$
    $\exists\, t \in \text{DOMAIN } ready\_q :$
    $\exists\, k \in \text{DOMAIN } cpus :$
    $\land\ cpus[k] = \text{""}$
    $\land\ cpus' = [cpus \text{ EXCEPT } ![k] = Head(ready\_q)]$
    $\land\ ready\_q' = Tail(ready\_q)$
    $\land\ \text{UNCHANGED } \langle lock\_owner,\ blocked\_q \rangle$
$Running \triangleq$
    $\exists\, k \in \text{DOMAIN } cpus :$
    $\lor\ MoveToReady(k)$
    $\lor\ Lock(k)$
    $\lor\ Unlock(k)$
$Next \triangleq$
    $\lor\ Running$
    $\lor\ Ready$

Next can update either a task that is running, or a task waiting to be scheduled.

A *Ready* task is popped off the ready queue and put onto an idle CPU. Since ready_q is implemented as an ordered tuple, fetching and popping the front is done using *Head* and *Tail*, respectively.

A *Running* task can either go back to the ready queue (done for now), acquire the global lock, or release the global lock. The sub-actions are defined below:

$MoveToReady(k) \triangleq$
    $\land\ cpus[k] \neq \text{""}$
    $\land\ lock\_owner \neq cpus[k]$
    $\land\ ready\_q' = Append(ready\_q,\ cpus[k])$
    $\land\ cpus' = [cpus \text{ EXCEPT } ![k] = \text{""}]$

$\wedge$ UNCHANGED $\langle lock\_owner,\ blocked\_q,\ blocked \rangle$

MoveToReady defines the where task voluntarily goes back to the ready queue.

$Lock(k) \triangleq$
$\vee \quad \wedge cpus[k] \neq$ ""
$\quad \wedge lock\_owner =$ ""
$\quad \wedge lock\_owner' = cpus[k]$
$\quad \wedge$ UNCHANGED $\langle ready\_q,\ cpus,\ blocked\_q,\ blocked \rangle$
$\vee \quad \wedge cpus[k] \neq$ ""
$\quad \wedge lock\_owner \neq$ ""
$\quad \wedge lock\_owner \neq cpus[k]$ $\quad$ cannot double lock
$\quad \wedge blocked\_q' = Append(blocked\_q,\ cpus[k])$
$\quad \wedge blocked' = [blocked$ EXCEPT $![cpus[k]] = 1]$
$\quad \wedge cpus' = [cpus$ EXCEPT $![k] =$ ""$]$
$\quad \wedge$ UNCHANGED $\langle ready\_q,\ lock\_owner \rangle$

Lock represents when a running task attempts to acquire the global lock. When the lock is free, the task grabs the lock and moves on. When the lock is already held, the task moves into the blocked queue to be scheduled when the lock is released. If multiple tasks attempt to acquire the lock while the lock is being held, the tasks will be inserted in the block queue in request order.

$Unlock(k) \triangleq$
$\quad \vee \quad \wedge cpus[k] \neq$ ""
$\quad\quad \wedge Len(blocked\_q) \neq 0$
$\quad\quad \wedge lock\_owner = cpus[k]$
$\quad\quad \wedge lock\_owner' = Head(blocked\_q)$
$\quad\quad \wedge cpus' = [cpus$ EXCEPT $![k] = Head(blocked\_q)]$
$\quad\quad \wedge ready\_q' = ready\_q \circ \langle cpus[k] \rangle$
$\quad\quad \wedge blocked\_q' = Tail(blocked\_q)$
$\quad\quad \wedge blocked' = [blocked$ EXCEPT $![Head(blocked\_q)] = 0]$
$\quad \vee \quad \wedge cpus[k] \neq$ ""
$\quad\quad \wedge Len(blocked\_q) = 0$
$\quad\quad \wedge lock\_owner' =$ ""

$\wedge$ UNCHANGED $\langle ready\_q,\ blocked\_q,\ blocked,\ cpus \rangle$

Unlock represents when a running task releases the lock. If there are no blocked tasks, the running task carries on as before. If there are blocked tasks, the first blocked task is scheduled to run immediately, and the running task is inserted at the end of the ready queue.

5.3 Safety

We can define safety properties to detect programmatic failures. For example: if a task is running on a CPU, this *implies* task cannot be blocked:

$Safety\ \triangleq$
    $\forall\, t \in\ Tasks:$
      $\forall\, k \in 0\,..\,N-1:$
      $cpus[k] = t \Rightarrow blocked[t] = 0$

5.4 Liveness

Any tasks attempting to acquire the lock when the lock is already taken become blocked. A liveness property we can define is to check the scheduler guarantee any blocked task eventually acquires the lock and run. Before we describe this liveness property, we need to first make sure no task can *cannot* hold onto the lock indefinitely (which is something the model checker *will try*):

$Fairness\ \triangleq$
    $\forall\, t \in\ Tasks:$
      $\forall\, n \in 0\,..\,(N-1):$
      $\mathrm{WF}_{vars}(HoldingLock(t) \wedge Unlock(n))$
$Spec\ \triangleq$
    $\wedge\ Init$
    $\wedge\ \Box[Next]_{vars}$
    $\wedge\ \mathrm{WF}_{vars}(Next)$
    $\wedge\ Fairness$

The weakness fairness description states that if the enabling condition for *HoldingLock* and *Unlock* continuously stays true (eg. a lock is being held and the task can unlock), the associated action, *Unlock*, must *always eventually* be called to satisfy the weak fairness requirement. We can now define the liveness property: a task blocked waiting for the lock *leads to* the task acquiring the lock:

$Liveness \triangleq$
$\quad \forall\, t \in Tasks :$
$\quad blocked[t] = 1 \rightsquigarrow lock\_owner = t$

Chapter 6

Simple Gossip Protocol

In a distributed system, a cluster of servers collectively provides a service. A distributed system may have 10s to 100s of servers working together to offer the service in a geo-diverse environment to maximize uptime. The servers often have requirements to know about each other. In the context of a distributed database, a server may need to know the key range of another of its peers. The cluster needs a way to communicate this information. One such mechanism is the gossip protocol.

Gossip protocol allows servers to fetch the latest cluster information in a distributed fashion. Before the gossip protocol, servers in a cluster learn about their neighbors by contacting a centralized server. This introduces a single failure point in the system. Gossip protocol relies on servers to initiate the data exchange, and the servers in the cluster periodically select a set of neighbors to gossip with.

Assume an N server cluster, at some periodic interval a server selects k neighbors to gossip with. The total amount of gossip propagation time is described logarithmically below:

$$propagation\_time = \log_k N * gossip\_interval$$

With the total number of messages exchanged:

$$messages\_exchanged = \log_k N * k$$

The following represents the state graph of a three node cluster running gossip protocol:

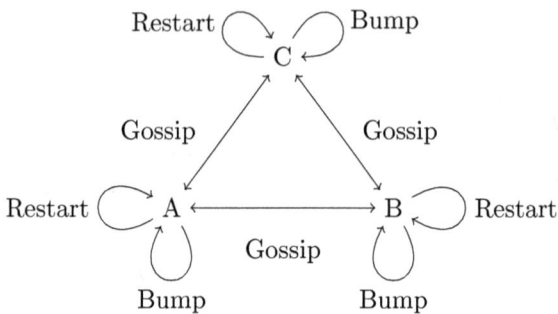

6.1   Design

In this chapter, we will implement a simplified gossip model where:

- Each server has a version.

- Each server caches the version of all other servers.

- A pair of servers are randomly selected to gossip.

- A server can restart. Restarting a server clears the server's version cache of the other servers.

- A server can bump its version.

If the gossip protocol works correctly, every server should eventually have the latest version of all the servers.

6.2   specification

In gossip protocol, every server needs to remember all its peer's current version:

$Init \triangleq$
    $\wedge\ version = [i \in Servers \mapsto [j \in Servers \mapsto 0]]$
$Next \triangleq$
    $\vee\ \exists\, i \in Servers :$
    $\wedge\ Bump(i)$
    $\vee\ \exists\, i,\, j \in Servers :$
    $\wedge\ Gossip(i,\, j)$
    $\vee\ \exists\, i \in Servers :$
    $\wedge\ Restart(i)$

The *Init* formula simply declares the version to be a two-dimensional array with all elements initialized to 0. *Next* allows either bumping the version of a server, picking a pair of servers to gossip, or restarting a server.

The following defines these steps:

$Gossip(i,\, j) \triangleq$
    LET
        $Max(a,\, b) \triangleq$ IF $a > b$ THEN a ELSE b
        $updated \triangleq [k \in Servers \mapsto Max(version[i][k],\ version[j][k])]$
        $version\_a \triangleq [version$ EXCEPT $![i] = updated]$
        $version\_ab \triangleq [version\_a$ EXCEPT $![j] = updated]$
    IN
        $\wedge\ version' = version\_ab$

When two servers gossip, they gossip about all the servers (including themselves) and update both of their version cache with the more up-to-date entry between the two. The *LET..IN* syntax enables local macro definition. In this example, we use temporary variables defined inside *LET*, and update the primed variable inside the *IN* clause.

$Bump(i) \triangleq$
$\wedge\ version[i][i] \neq MaxVersion$
$\wedge\ version' = [version$ EXCEPT $![i] = [k \in Servers \mapsto$
IF $i \neq k$ THEN $version[i][k]$ ELSE $version[i][k] + 1]]$

Bump only increments the version if the server hasn't made it to *MaxVersion*. When the Server bumps the version, it only bumps its version and keeps all other versions in its version cache as is.

$Restart(i) \triangleq$
$\qquad \wedge version' = [version$ EXCEPT $![i] = [k \in Servers \mapsto$
$\qquad$ IF $i \neq k$ THEN 0 ELSE $version[i][i]]]$

Upon *Restart*, a server reloads from its local storage (so its version persists), but the server needs to re-learn the cluster status (all other entries in its version cache are wiped).

6.3 Safety

One safety property is to confirm *all* version values are within bounds:

$Safety \triangleq$
$\qquad \forall i, j \in Servers :$
$\qquad \wedge version[i][j] \geq 0$
$\qquad \wedge version[i][j] \leq MaxVersion$

This can be read as: for all possible pairs of servers i and j, the value of *version[i][j]* must be within 0 and *MaxVersion*, inclusive.

6.4 Liveness

Spec defines three actions: *Bump, Restart, Gossip*. Without any fairness description, *Any* permutation of these actions are allowed by *Spec*, including:

- Restart, Restart, Restart,...

- Restart, Gossip, Restart, Gossip, ...

- Gossip, Gossip, Gossip, ...

Some of these are not of interest (eg. the cluster is stuck in a loop where node is constantly restarting). In the gossip protocol, we are interested in verifying the cluster over time converges towards higher version value for all servers. This means we need to make sure *Bump* is guaranteed to be called under some circumstances. This is where the fairness description comes in. To ensure *Bump* is always called:

$$Spec \triangleq$$
$$\land\ Init$$
$$\land\ \Box[Next]_{vars}$$
$$\land\ \mathrm{WF}_{vars}(Next)$$
$$\land\ \forall\, i \in Servers:$$
$$\quad \mathrm{WF}_{vars}(Bump(i))$$

The model checker explores all possible transitions permitted by *Spec*, including calling any subset of actions repeatedly. Fairness description guarantees that if the enabling condition of an action is true, the action will be taken. If the system is trapped in a *Restart* and *Gossip* loop when *Bump* can be called, specifying fairness for *Bump* ensures *Bump* is called, breaking the loop.

With *Spec* ensuring the system always migrate towards higher version number, we can now define the Liveness property:

$$Liveness \triangleq$$
$$\quad \exists\, i, j \in Servers:$$
$$\quad \land\ i \neq j$$
$$\quad \land\ \Box\Diamond(\ \land\ version[i][i]\ = MaxVersion$$
$$\quad\ \land\ version[i][j] = MaxVersion$$
$$\quad\ \land\ version[j][i] = MaxVersion$$
$$\quad\ \land\ version[j][j] = MaxVersion)$$

The $\Box\Diamond$ represents *always eventually*. The liveness condition specifies that there exists a pair of Servers such that both of them *always eventually* make it to *MaxVersion* and have *Gossip* with each other.

Since *Spec* permits *Restart* to be called anytime, a liveness property where *all* Servers are up-to-date cannot be true. The model checker can always *Restart* one of the Servers before this property is met.

Likewise, replacing *always eventually* with *eventually always* ($\Diamond\Box$) also fails. $\Diamond\Box$ checks that once the system *eventually* enters a specified state, it *always* remains in that state. This cannot be true as the liveness condition is transient, since the model checker can always disturb any condition with a *Restart*.

For a more comprehensive discussion of fairness, please refer to Chapter 15.

Chapter 7

Selective Retransmit

Assume a client device that plays a video stream. Structurally, a video is composed of frames, frames are then segmented into packets to stream across a network. The client device recombines the packets into a frame and then sequences the frame to playback the video.

However, the network is not-deterministic. Depending on the route the packets take to get to the client, they may arrive out-of-order. The client may need to maintain a receive buffer for the packets and re-order the packets back into sequence before pushing the packets down to the decoding engine.

The network may also drop packets if any of the switches along the way get busy. In the case of a packet drop, the client has a few options. The client can either discard the frame and let the decoding engine downstream deal with it (which may result in visible artifacts during playback). The client can request the whole frame to be re-sent, which results in additional bandwidth consumption. The client can selectively request the missing packet to be retransmitted, which will minimize additional bandwidth consumption but increase implementation complexity.

In this chapter, we will implement a simple selective retransmit algorithm.

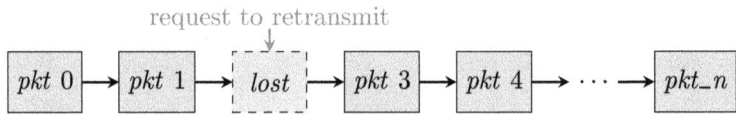

Since packets may arrive out-of-order, the server stamps the packets with sequence numbers to allow the client to order the packets as they arrive. Once the client has a set of ordered packets, it moves the packets from the receive buffer into the decoding engine to be displayed.

The video packets are often sent via unreliable channels to minimize network overhead and latency. The client sends an acknowledgement back to the server to acknowledge the received packet. This indicates to the server it can send more video data to the client. Acknowledgements are not latency-sensitive and take up a very small proportion of bandwidth, so they are transported through reliable channels.

The following illustrates packet reorder handling:

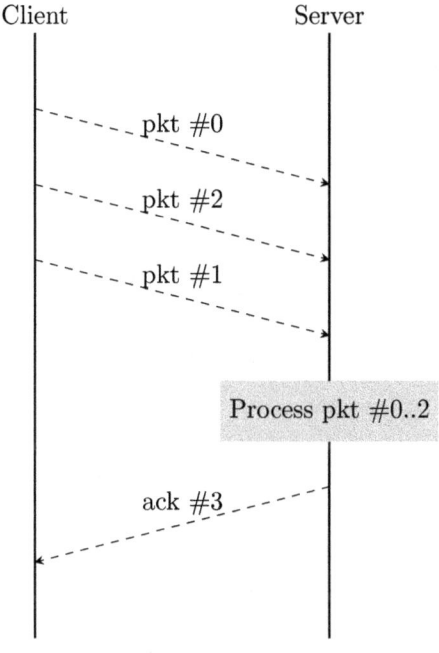

The following illustrates packet loss handling:

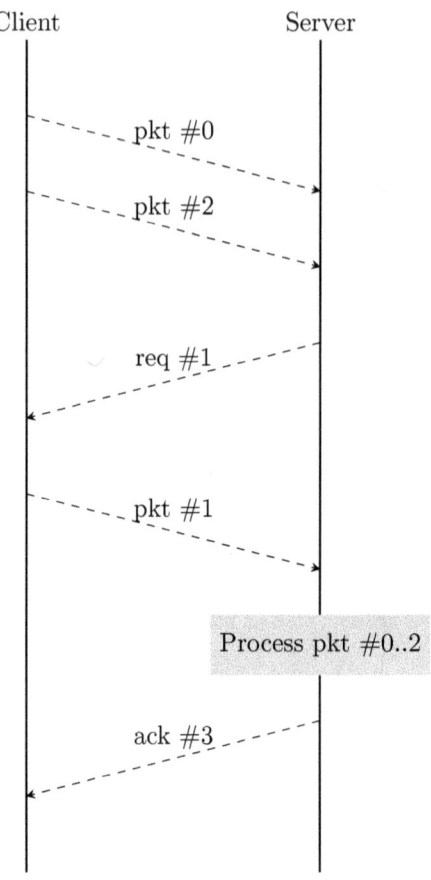

There are other design considerations. The server is allowed to send up to W packets before getting an acknowledgement, this reduces latency perceived by the user. The client also doesn't need to acknowledge all the packets, since the server assumes once an acknowledgement of packet N is received, then all packets before N has also been received.

7.1 Design

With the above description, we are now ready to provide a more formal description of our design:

- Client is the receiver that displays the video stream.

- Server is the sender that sends the video stream.

- Server always sends the packets in order.

- Client may receive the packets out-of-order.

- Client may never receive some packet due to loss.

- Server can send up to W packets before an acknowledgement is received

- Packet sequence number is represented by a fixed number of bytes in the network header, the sequence number will eventually wrap around once it hits the maximum representable value. The maximum sequence number is represented as N-1.

- Client puts a received packet in its receive buffer. Packets in the receive buffer may be out-of-order due to network conditions.

- Client will remove the packets from the receive buffer once the sequence number of the received packets is contiguous. The client will also send an acknowledgement back to the Server with the most recently acknowledged sequence number.

- Data packets are transported using unreliable channels due to bandwidth and latency requirements.

- Control packets are transported using reliable channels due to relaxed and latency requirements.

We are now ready to implement the specification.

7.2   specification

The following is the skeleton of the Spec:

$Init \triangleq$
$\quad \wedge network = \{\}$
$\quad \wedge server\_tx = 0$
$\quad \wedge server\_tx\_limit = W$
$\quad \wedge server\_tx\_ack = 0$
$\quad \wedge client\_rx = 0$
$\quad \wedge client\_buffer = \{\}$
$\quad \wedge lost = 0$

$Next \triangleq$
$\quad \vee Send$
$\quad \vee \exists p \in network :$
$\quad Receive(p)$
$\quad \vee ClientRetransmitRequest$
$\quad \vee ClientAcknowledgement$
$\quad \vee \exists p \in network :$
$\quad \wedge p.dst = $ "client"
$\quad \wedge Drop(p)$

The server is represented by three variables:

- $tx+1$ represents the sequence number to be used in the next packet

- tx_limit represents the highest sequence number the server can send without waiting for an acknowledgement

- tx_ack represents the most recent acknowledged sequence number

The client is represented by two variables:

- $client\_rx$ is the most recently acknowledged sequence number

- $client\_buffer$ is the receive buffer holding all the packets waiting to be re-ordered before being acknowledged

The allowed actions include packet *Receive*, which the existential quantifier also has the side effect of re-ordering. *ClientRetransmitRequest* detects and sends retransmit requests. *ClientAcknowledgement* sends acknowledgement. Finally, data packets may be dropped.

Before we start defining the actions, let us define some helper functions:

$MinS(s) \triangleq$
CHOOSE $x \in s : \forall\, y \in s : x \leq y$

$MaxS(s) \triangleq$
CHOOSE $x \in s : \forall\, y \in s : x \geq y$

$MaxIndex \triangleq$
    LET
        $upper \triangleq \{x \in client\_buffer : x > N - W\}$
        $lower \triangleq \{x \in client\_buffer : x < W\}$
        $maxv \triangleq$ IF $upper \neq \{\} \wedge lower \neq \{\}$
          THEN
            $MaxS(lower)$
          ELSE
            $MaxS(client\_buffer)$
    IN
       $maxv$

$MinIndex \triangleq$
    LET
        $upper \triangleq \{x \in client\_buffer : x > N - W\}$
        $lower \triangleq \{x \in client\_buffer : x < W\}$
        $minv \triangleq$ IF $upper \neq \{\} \wedge lower \neq \{\}$
          THEN
            $MinS(upper)$
          ELSE
            $MinS(client\_buffer)$
    IN
       $minv$

$Range \triangleq$

IF $MaxIndex \geq MinIndex$
   THEN
      $MaxIndex - MinIndex + 1$
   ELSE
      $MaxIndex + 1 + N - MinIndex$

At any moment the system allows a window of packets to be un-acknowledged. Both the client and server are aware of the window size, represented by W. By looking at packets in its receive buffer and its most recently acknowledged sequence number, the client can determine which packets were lost.

There's some nuisance to implement this. Since the system does not allow more than W unacknowledged packets, the client can assume the window of the packet in its receiver buffer must have sequence number $s \in client\_rx..client\_rx + W$. Since the sequence number has a ceiling, the window of packets may wrap around the boundary. This introduces some complications around determining the minimum and maximum in the window of the packet. The functions defined above calculate the range, maximum and minimum value in the window accounting for possible wrapped around.

Now we can look at how the client acknowledgement logic:

$MergeReady \triangleq$
   $\wedge \; client\_buffer \neq \{\}$
   $\wedge \; (client\_rx + 1)\%N = MinIndex$ contiguous with previous ack
   $\wedge \; Range = Cardinality(client\_buffer)$ combined is contiguous

$ClientAcknowledgement \triangleq$
   $\wedge \; client\_buffer \neq \{\}$
   $\wedge \; MergeReady$
   $\wedge \; client\_buffer' = \{\}$
   $\wedge \; client\_rx' = MaxIndex$
   $\wedge \; network' = AddMessage([dst \mapsto \text{"server"},$
$type \mapsto \text{"ack"},$
$ack \mapsto MaxIndex],$
   $network)$

$\land$ UNCHANGED $\langle$ *server_tx*, *server_tx_ack*, *server_tx_limit*, *lost* $\rangle$

The client only acknowledges when it has a contiguous sequence of packets that follows its most recently acknowledged packet. When MergeReady is true, the client sends the acknowledgement back to the server.

$ClientReceive(pp) \;\triangleq$
 $\land$ *network′* = *RemoveMessage(pp, network)*
 $\land$ *client_buffer′* = *client_buffer* $\cup$ $\{pp.seq\}$
 $\land$ UNCHANGED $\langle$ *server_tx*, *client_rx*,
 server_tx_ack, *server_tx_limit*, *lost* $\rangle$

$Missing \;\triangleq$
 LET
  $full\_seq \;\triangleq$
   IF *MaxIndex* $\geq$ *client_rx* + 1
    THEN
     $\{x \in client\_rx + 1 \,..\, MaxIndex : \text{TRUE}\}$
    ELSE
     $\{x \in 0 \,..\, MaxIndex : \text{TRUE}\} \cup \{x \in client\_rx + 1 \,..\, N - 1 : \text{TRUE}\}$
  $all\_client\_msgs \;\triangleq\; \{m \in network : m.dst = \text{"client"}\}$
  $all\_client\_seqs \;\triangleq\; \{m.seq : m \in all\_client\_msgs\}$
  $network\_missing \;\triangleq\; full\_seq \setminus all\_client\_seqs$
  $client\_missing \;\triangleq\; full\_seq \setminus client\_buffer$
  $to\_request \;\triangleq\; network\_missing \cap client\_missing$
 IN
  $to\_request$

$ClientRetransmitRequest \;\triangleq$
 $\land$ $\neg MergeReady$
 $\land$ *client_buffer* $\neq$ $\{\}$
 $\land$ *Missing* $\neq$ $\{\}$
 $\land$ *network′* = *AddMessage(*[*dst* $\mapsto$ "server",
 type $\mapsto$ "retransmit",
 seq $\mapsto$ CHOOSE $x \in Missing : \text{TRUE}$],
  network)
 $\land$ UNCHANGED $\langle$ *server_tx*, *server_tx_limit*,

$client\_rx,\ client\_buffer,\ server\_tx\_ack,\ lost\rangle$

ClientReceive moves the packet from the network into the client receive buffer. The only reason why this is done as a separate step is to make debugging easier.

Missing returns a set of missing missing sequence numbers. This is done by cross-checking the client receive buffer and the outstanding network packet targeting the client. In theory, the client doesn't know if a gap in its receive buffer means the packet is lost or will arrive soon. Practically, the client will assume a packet is lost after some configurable timeout and request a retransmit.

Let us take a look at server-related definitions:

$RemoveStaleAck(ack,\ msgs)\ \triangleq$
    LET
          $acks\ \triangleq\ \{(ack - k + N)\%N : k \in 1\ ..\ W\}$
    IN
        $\{m \in msgs : \neg(\wedge\ m.dst = \text{"server"}$
              $\wedge\ m.type = \text{"ack"}$
              $\wedge\ m.ack \in acks)\}$

$ServerReceive(pp)\ \triangleq$
    $\vee\ \wedge\ pp.type = \text{"ack"}$
    $\wedge\ server\_tx\_ack' = pp.ack$
    $\wedge\ server\_tx\_limit' = (pp.ack + W)\%N$
    $\wedge\ network' = RemoveStaleAck(pp.ack,$
    $RemoveMessage(pp,\ network))$
    $\wedge$ UNCHANGED $\langle server\_tx,\ client\_rx,\ client\_buffer,\ lost\rangle$
    $\vee\ \wedge\ pp.type = \text{"retransmit"}$
    $\wedge\ network' = AddMessage([dst \mapsto \text{"client"},\ seq \mapsto pp.seq],$
    $RemoveMessage(pp,\ network))$
    $\wedge\ lost' = lost - 1$
    $\wedge$ UNCHANGED $\langle server\_tx,\ server\_tx\_limit,$
      $client\_rx,\ client\_buffer,\ server\_tx\_ack\rangle$

When the server receives an acknowledgement for sequence number K, it assumes K-1 and prior were all received by the client. *RemoveStaleAck* is a model optimization to drop all acknowledgements with sequence numbers less than K. Note that sequence numbers k, k-N, and k-2*N, are all represented as k, and intheory, the client may not be able to differentiate between them. Practically, N is sized large enough to represent a few second's worth of data, so the system can safely assume a sequence number k is for the most recent N packets.

Upon receiving an acknowledgement from the client, the server bumps the server_tx_limit allowing it to send more data. The server can also receive a retransmit request and send the requested data. *lost* is configurable to determine how many packets can be dropped at the same time.

7.3   Model Simplification

7.3.1   Removing Stale Acknowlegement

When the server acknowledges K, it has already received all the packets before K. Likewise, when the client receives an acknowledgement for K, it can assume all previous packets have been received. The client may receive the acknowledgement out-of-order due to unfavourable network conditions. One reduction we can make to the model is simply *remove all stale acknowledgements*. In a practical implementation, this is also how the client can react when it receives stale acknowledgements.

There is a bit of nuisance here. Since the sequence number wraps around, the client cannot differentiate between K from K-N, K-2*N, etc. However, N is usually large enough to accommodate a few seconds of data before a sequence number is re-used. The client can be confident that any K received the current K, not K-N or earlier.

7.3.2   Retransmit Request Assumed Reliable

Retransmit requests packets can be delivered through unreliable channels. However, this makes no difference in the model. The client sends a retransmit request when it detects packets are lost. If the model drops the retransmit request, the client will just send another retransmit request because the missing packet is still missing.

While this can be modeled, it would increase the runtime without providing many benefits. For this Spec, we simply assume all control packets are reliable.

7.4 Safety

Omitted for this chapter.

7.5 Liveness

Given the system may randomly drop packets, one possible liveness condition is to verify packets of all sequence numbers are received by the client at some point. This can be described as for all possible sequence number value k, k is eventually exists in the client receive buffer.

$Liveness \triangleq$
$\quad \forall i \in 0 .. N-1 :$
$\quad client\_buffer = \{\} \rightsquigarrow \exists j \in client\_buffer : i = j$

Chapter 8

BitTorrent Protocol

BitTorrent is a peer-to-peer file-sharing protocol that allows nodes to distribute data in a decentralized fashion. The tracker is the central server that knows all the members in the cluster. A node coming online learns about its peers by talking to the tracker. Once a node learns about the peer nodes, the node can initiate data exchange with its peers directly. Files are exchanged in chunks, and a node will contact its peers to determine who has data it doesn't have.

The following is a BitTorrent cluster with five nodes:

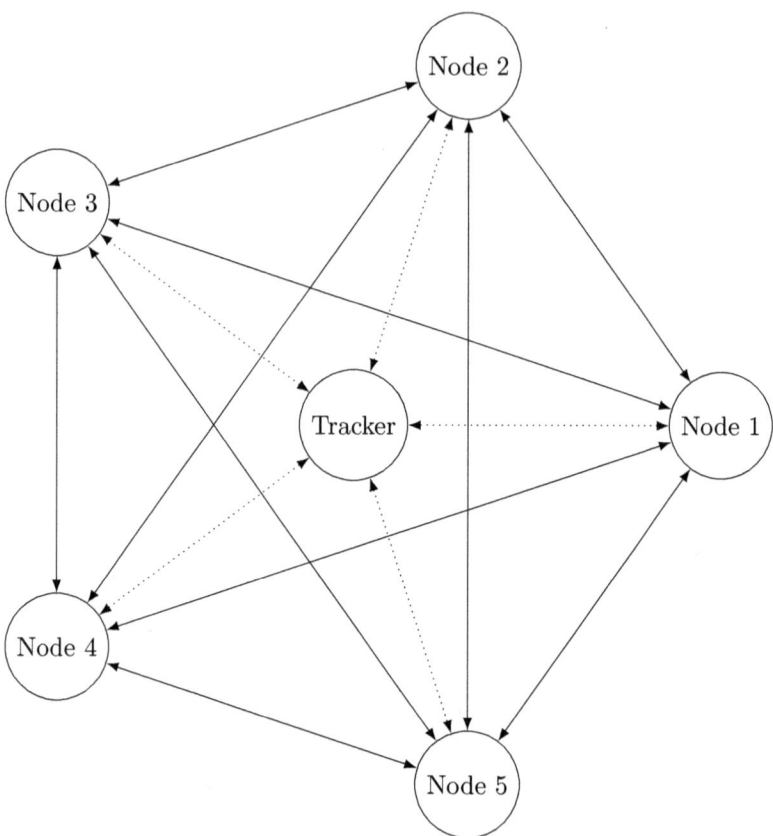

8.1   Design

In this chapter, we will implement a simple BitTorrent cluster. The cluster will have a single tracker and N nodes. A node can join or leave the cluster, and make progress while inside the cluster.

To simplify the model, we assume a single file with N chunks is shared within the cluster. We also assume at any moment the cluster contains the entire file. This means while a node can leave the cluster at any time, it can only leave if the cluster still has the entire file after it leaves.

8.2   specification

The cluster starts with a single *Seed* node that has the entire data set. In every step, a node can *Join, Progress,* or *Leave.*

$Init \triangleq$
    $\land\ tracker = \{Seed\}$
    $\land\ data = [k \in Client \mapsto \text{IF } k = Seed \text{ THEN } AllChunks \text{ ELSE } \{\}]$

$Next \triangleq$
    $\lor\ \exists\, k \in Client :$
    $Join(k)$
    $\lor\ \exists\, k \in Client :$
    $Progress(k)$
    $\lor\ \exists\, k \in Client :$
    $Leave(k)$

A node can join a cluster if it's not currently part of it:

$Join(k) \triangleq$
$\land\ k \notin tracker$
$\land\ tracker' = tracker \cup \{k\}$
$\land\ \text{UNCHANGED } data$

A node can leave a cluster. To simplify the model, a node k can leave if and only if the cluster still has the full data set without k. A node can *Leave* even if it doesn't have the entire file:

$AllDataWithout(k) \triangleq$
    $\text{UNION } \{data[i] : i \in tracker \setminus \{k\}\}$

$Leave(k) \triangleq$
    $\land\ k \in tracker$
    $\land\ AllDataWithout(k) = AllChunks$

$$\land \ tracker' = tracker \setminus \{k\}$$
$$\land \ data' = [data \ \text{EXCEPT} \ ![k] = \{\}]$$

Finally, for a node U to make progress: U must have an incomplete set of data and there's another node V that has data U doesn't have:

$Progress(u) \ \triangleq$
    $\land \ u \in tracker$
    $\land \ data[u] \neq AllChunks$ u is incomplete
    $\land \ \exists \ v \in tracker :$
    $\exists \ k \in AllChunks :$
        $\land \ k \notin data[u]$ v has something u doesn't
        $\land \ k \in data[v]$
        $\land \ data' = [data \ \text{EXCEPT} \ ![u] = data[u] \cup \{k\}]$
        $\land \ \text{UNCHANGED} \ tracker$

8.3 Safety

A requirement we imposed on the design is to ensure the cluster contains the entire file at all times:

$Safety \ \triangleq$
    $\text{UNION} \ \{data[k] : k \in Client\} = AllChunks$

8.4 Liveness

We want to verify a newly joined node eventually gets the entire file. However, verifying *all* nodes eventually get the whole file will take too long. We will define the check liveness property for only one node:

$NodeToVerify \ \triangleq \ \text{``c0''}$

$Liveness \ \triangleq$
    targeted liveness condition
    $data[NodeToVerify] = \{\} \rightsquigarrow data[NodeToVerify] = AllChunks$

The liveness property checks for a node with no data and eventually gets all the data.

$Spec \triangleq$

$\quad \wedge\ Init$

$\quad \wedge\ \Box[Next]_{vars}$

$\quad \wedge\ \mathrm{WF}_{vars}(Next)$

$\quad$ targeted fairness description

$\quad \wedge\ \mathrm{SF}_{vars}(Join(NodeToVerify))$

$\quad \wedge\ \forall\, s\ \in\ \textsc{subset}\ AllChunks :$

$\quad\quad \mathrm{SF}_{vars}(data[NodeToVerify] = s \wedge Progress(NodeToVerify))$

Without fairness, *Spec* permits a node to *never* make progress by having it repeatedly join and leave the cluster. To ensure *NodeToVerify* always makes progress, we need to enable strong fairness for *Progress*. However, this alone is not enough. We need to ensure *Progress* is called for *all* possible *NodeToVerify* state, this is solved using the *SUBSET* keyword.

Chapter 9

Raft Consensus Protocol

Raft is a consensus algorithm that enables a cluster of nodes to agree on a collective state even in the presence of failures. An application of Raft is a database replication protocol. With a replication factor of 3 (eg. data is replicated across 3 nodes) and a hard drive failure rate of 0.81% per year, the possibility of total failure where the entire replication group goes down is $1 - 0.0081^3 = 99.9999\%$ uptime [6].

This chapter implements only the leader election portion of the protocol to limit the scope of the discussion. For a full description of the Raft protocol, please refer to the original paper [7].

9.1 Design

We will briefly describe Raft and its leadership election process below:

- A Raft cluster has N nodes, the cluster works collectively as a *system* to offer some service

- Each node can be in one of three possible states: Follower, Candidate, Leader

- During normal operations, a cluster of N nodes has a single leader and N-1 followers

- The leader handles all the client interactions. Requests sent to followers will be redirected to the leader

- The leader regularly sends a heartbeat to the follower, indicating its alive

- If a follower fails to receive a heartbeat from the leader after timeout, it will become a candidate, vote for itself, and campaign to be leader

- A candidate who collects the majority of the vote becomes the leader

- If multiple candidates are campaigning and a split vote happens, candidates will eventually declare an election timeout and start a new round of election

- The cluster can have multiple leaders due to unfavorable network conditions, but the leaders must be on different terms

- A newly elected leader will send a heartbeat to other nodes to establish leadership

- All requests and responses include the sender's term, allowing the receiver to react accordingly

The protocol also included a description of log synchronization, state recovery, and more. Many details are omitted in this chapter to reduce modeling costs. The N nodes in the cluster operate *independently* following the above heuristics. Hopefully, this highlights the complexity of verifying the correctness of the protocol.

The following illustrates the state diagram of one node in the cluster:

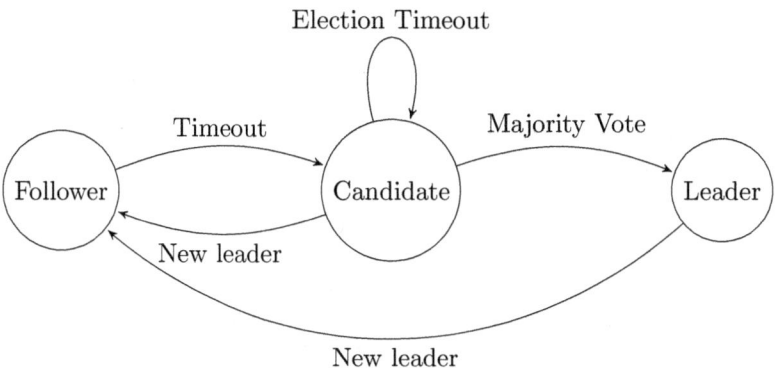

9.2 Specification

The following implements the skeleton portion of the leader election protocol:

$Init \triangleq$
$\quad\quad \land state = [s \in Servers \mapsto \text{"Follower"}]$
$\quad\quad \land messages = \{\}$
$\quad\quad \land voted\_for = [s \in Servers \mapsto \text{""}]$
$\quad\quad \land vote\_granted = [s \in Servers \mapsto \{\}]$
$\quad\quad \land vote\_requested = [s \in Servers \mapsto 0]$
$\quad\quad \land term = [s \in Servers \mapsto 0]$

$RequestVoteSet(i) \triangleq \{$
$\quad [fSrc \mapsto i, fDst \mapsto s, fType \mapsto \text{"RequestVoteReq"}, fTerm \mapsto term[i]]$
$\quad\quad : s \in Servers \setminus \{i\}$
$\}$

$Campaign(i) \triangleq$
$\quad\quad \land vote\_requested[i] = 0$
$\quad\quad \land vote\_requested' = [vote\_requested \text{ EXCEPT } ![i] = 1]$
$\quad\quad \land messages' = messages \cup RequestVoteSet(i)$
$\quad\quad \land \text{UNCHANGED } \langle state, term, vote\_granted, voted\_for \rangle$

$KeepAliveSet(i) \triangleq \{$

$[fSrc \mapsto i, fDst \mapsto s, fType \mapsto$ "AppendEntryReq", $fTerm \mapsto term[i]]$
$: s \in Servers \setminus \{i\}$
$\}$

$Leader(i) \triangleq$
$\quad \wedge state[i] =$ "Leader"
$\quad \wedge messages' = messages \cup KeepAliveSet(i)$
$\quad \wedge$ UNCHANGED $\langle state, voted\_for, term, vote\_granted, vote\_requested \rangle$

$BecomeLeader(i) \triangleq$
$\quad \wedge Cardinality(vote\_granted[i]) > Cardinality(Servers) \div 2$
$\quad \wedge state' = [state$ EXCEPT $![i] =$ "Leader"$]$
$\quad \wedge$ UNCHANGED $\langle messages, voted\_for,$
$\quad term, vote\_granted, vote\_requested \rangle$

$Candidate(i) \triangleq$
$\quad \wedge state[i] =$ "Candidate"
$\quad \wedge \vee Campaign(i)$
$\quad \vee BecomeLeader(i)$
$\quad \vee Timeout(i)$

$Follower(i) \triangleq$
$\quad \wedge state[i] =$ "Follower"
$\quad \wedge Timeout(i)$

$Receive(msg) \triangleq$
$\quad \vee \wedge msg.fType =$ "AppendEntryReq"
$\quad \wedge AppendEntryReq(msg)$
$\quad \vee \wedge msg.fType =$ "AppendEntryResp"
$\quad \wedge AppendEntryResp(msg)$
$\quad \vee \wedge msg.fType =$ "RequestVoteReq"
$\quad \wedge RequestVoteReq(msg)$
$\quad \vee \wedge msg.fType =$ "RequestVoteResp"
$\quad \wedge RequestVoteResp(msg)$

$Next \triangleq$
$\quad \vee \exists i \in Servers :$
$\quad \vee Leader(i)$
$\quad \vee Candidate(i)$
$\quad \vee Follower(i)$

$\lor \exists\, msg \in messages : Receive(msg)$

- *Next* either picks a server to make progress, or picks a message in the message pool to process. Message processing is done by *Receive*, handling is state agnostic

- *message* is defined to be a set that holds a collection of functions, where each function is a message with source, destination, type, and more specified

- *voted_for* tracks who a given node previously voted for. This prevents a node from voting more than once

- *vote_granted* tracks how many votes a candidate has received

- *vote_requested* tracks if a node has already issued a request vote to its peers

- *Follower* either Receive or Timeout and campaign to be a leader

- *Candidate* campaigns to be a leader, and becomes one if it has enough vote. Failing to collect enough votes, *Candidate* start a new election on a new term. It can also receive a request with a higher term and transition to be a *Follower*.

- *Leader* will establish its leadership by sending *AppepndEntryReq* to all its peers

Spec implements four messages AppendEntry request/response, RequestVote request/response. Handling for all messages is similar in structure. In this chapter, we will look at *RequestVoteReq* only. Readers are encouraged to check the remaining definition as an exercise:

$RequestVoteReq(msg) \triangleq$
    LET
        $i \triangleq msg.fDst$
        $j \triangleq msg.fSrc$
        $type \triangleq msg.fType$
        $t \triangleq msg.fTerm$
    IN

haven't voted, or whom we voted re-requested

$\vee \wedge t = term[i]$

$\wedge \vee voted\_for[i] = j$

$\vee voted_for[i] = $ ""

$\wedge voted\_for' = [voted\_for \text{ EXCEPT } ![i] = j]$

$\wedge messages' = AddMessage([fSrc \mapsto i,$

$fDst \mapsto j,$

$fType \mapsto$ "RequestVoteResp",

$fTerm \mapsto t,$

$fSuccess \mapsto 1],$

$RemoveMessage(msg, messages))$

$\wedge$ UNCHANGED $\langle state, term, vote\_granted,$

$vote\_requested, establish\_leadership\rangle$

already voted for someone else

$\vee \wedge t = term[i]$

$\wedge voted\_for[i] \neq j$

$\wedge voted_for[i] \neq $ ""

$\wedge messages' = AddMessage([fSrc \mapsto i,$

$fDst \mapsto j,$

$fType \mapsto$ "RequestVoteResp",

$fTerm \mapsto t,$

$fSuccess \mapsto 0],$

$RemoveMessage(msg, messages))$

$\wedge$ UNCHANGED $\langle state, voted\_for, term,$

$vote\_granted, vote\_requested, establish\_leadership\rangle$

$\vee \wedge t < term[i]$

$\wedge messages' = AddMessage([fSrc \mapsto i,$

$fDst \mapsto j,$

$fType \mapsto$ "RequestVoteResp",

$fTerm \mapsto term[i],$

$fSuccess \mapsto 0],$

$RemoveMessage(msg, messages))$

$\wedge$ UNCHANGED $\langle state, voted\_for, term,$

$vote\_granted, vote\_requested, establish\_leadership\rangle$

revert to follower

$\vee \wedge t > term[i]$

$\wedge state' = [state \text{ EXCEPT } ![i] = $ "Follower"$]$

$\wedge term' = [term \text{ EXCEPT } ![i] = t]$

$$\land \mathit{voted\_for}' = [\mathit{voted\_for} \text{ EXCEPT } ![i] = j]$$
$$\land \mathit{vote\_granted}' = [\mathit{vote\_granted} \text{ EXCEPT } ![i] = \{\}]$$
$$\land \mathit{vote\_requested}' = [\mathit{vote\_requested} \text{ EXCEPT } ![i] = 0]$$
$$\land \mathit{establish\_leadership}' = [\mathit{establish\_leadership} \text{ EXCEPT } ![i] = 0]$$
$$\land \mathit{messages}' = \mathit{AddMessage}([\mathit{fSrc} \mapsto i,$$
$$\mathit{fDst} \mapsto j,$$
$$\mathit{fType} \mapsto \text{"RequestVoteResp"},$$
$$\mathit{fTerm} \mapsto t,$$
$$\mathit{fSuccess} \mapsto 1],$$
$$\mathit{RemoveMessage}(\mathit{msg},\ \mathit{messages}))$$

The handling is split into three cases:

- If the received request is on a higher term, the processing node grants a vote and becomes a Follower

- If the received request is on a lower term, the processing node ignores the request

- If the received request is on the same term, the processing node only grants vote if it hasn't voted, or has voted for the same requester prior

9.3 Model Simplication

The model checker will run *Spec* as defined but is unlikely to be completed in a reasonable amount of time due to exponential state growth. We need to simplify the model, and careful consideration must go into finding the right balance between maximizing model correctness and minimizing model checker runtime.

The main strategy is to *bound* the state graph. The following describes a set of optimizations implemented for this example.

9.3.1 Modeling Messages as a Set

In the original Raft TLA+ Spec [8], messages are modeled as an *unordered map* to track the count of each message. It is possible for a

sender to repeatedly send the same message (eg. keepalive), and grow
the message count in an unbounded fashion.

messages in this example has been implemented as a set, which
effectively limits the message instance count to one. It is still possible for messages to grow unboundedly because of the monotonically
increasing term value. More changes are described below.

9.3.2 Limit Term Divergence

It is possible for a node to *never* make progress. Such a case can occur
when a node is partitioned off while the rest of the cluster elects a new
leader and moves onto newer terms. Many of the interesting behaviors
of Raft are how it addresses these cases. In a cluster of nodes with
mixed terms, the nodes with older terms will eventually converge onto
newer terms when they are contacted by a new leader. This converg-
ing behavior will happen whether the stale node is either 1 or N terms
away from the current leader, and the former is much less costly to
simulate than the latter because of the reduced number of states.

We can include *LimitDivergence* as a conjunction in *Timeout*:

$LimitDivergence(i) \triangleq$
    LET
        $values \triangleq \{term[s] : s \in Servers\}$
        $max\_v \triangleq$ CHOOSE $x \in values : \forall y \in values : x \geq y$
        $min\_v \triangleq$ CHOOSE $x \in values : \forall y \in values : x \leq y$
    IN
        $\vee \wedge term[i] \neq max\_v$
        $\vee \wedge term[i] = max\_v$
        $\wedge term[i] - min\_v < MaxDiff$

$Timeout(i) \triangleq$
    $\wedge LimitDivergence(i)$
    $\wedge state' = [state$ EXCEPT $![i] =$ "Candidate"$]$
    $\wedge voted\_for' = [voted\_for$ EXCEPT $![i] = i]$ voted for myself
    $\wedge vote\_granted' = [vote\_granted$ EXCEPT $![i] = \{i\}]$
    $\wedge vote\_requested' = [vote\_requested$ EXCEPT $![i] = 0]$

$\land\ term' = [term\ \text{EXCEPT}\ ![i] = @ + 1]$ \hfill bump term
$\land\ establish\_leadership' = [establish\_leadership\ \text{EXCEPT}\ ![i] = 0]$
$\land\ \text{UNCHANGED}\ \langle messages \rangle$
/ PrintT(state')

9.3.3   Normalize Cluster Term

However, *term* can grow unbounded. A monotonically increasing counter is what many consensus protocols rely on to represent the latest reality. We want to *normalize* the range of terms in the cluster so the minimum value resets back to 0 to bound the state graph. This is a trick described in [9].

$Normalize\ \overset{\Delta}{=}$
    LET
        $values\ \overset{\Delta}{=}\ \{term[s] : s \in Servers\}$
        $max\_v\ \overset{\Delta}{=}\ \text{CHOOSE}\ x \in values : \forall\, y \in values : x \geq y$
        $min\_v\ \overset{\Delta}{=}\ \text{CHOOSE}\ x \in values : \forall\, y \in values : x \leq y$
    IN
        $\land\ max\_v = MaxTerm$
        $\land\ term' = [s \in Servers \mapsto term[s] - min\_v]$
        $\land\ messages' = \{\}$
        $\land\ \text{UNCHANGED}\ \langle state,\ voted\_for,$
        $vote\_granted,\ vote\_requested,\ establish\_leadership \rangle$

$Next\ \overset{\Delta}{=}$
    $\lor\ \land\ \forall\, i \in Servers : term[i] \neq MaxTerm$
    $\land\ \lor\ \exists\, i \in Servers :$
    $\lor\ Leader(i)$
    $\lor\ Candidate(i)$
    $\lor\ Follower(i)$
    $\lor\ \exists\, msg \in messages : Receive(msg)$
    $\lor\ \land\ \exists\, i \in Servers : term[i] = MaxTerm$
    $\land\ Normalize$

The implementation ensures only the state machine only moves forward when none of the nodes is on *MaxTerm*. If any of the nodes are on *MaxTerm*, the cluster terms are normalized.

Another caveat here is in the initial implementation I didn't update messages. This led to liveness property violation as the messages had terms disagreeing with the system state. To simplify *Spec* I simply cleared all messages. This indirectly verifies a portion of the packet loss handling in *Spec* as well.

9.3.4   Sending Request as a Batch

The send requests were initially implemented using the existential quantifier. This introduces many interleaving states. This was replaced with a universal quantifier so the set of messages is only sent once. The implementation no longer tracks if the responses were received since *Spec* should handle packet loss scenarios as well.

$RequestVoteSet(i) \triangleq \{$
 $[fSrc \mapsto i, fDst \mapsto s, fType \mapsto \text{``RequestVoteReq''}, fTerm \mapsto term[i]]$
  $: s \in Servers \setminus \{i\}$
$\}$

$Campaign(i) \triangleq$
 $\land vote\_requested[i] = 0$
 $\land vote\_requested' = [vote\_requested \text{ EXCEPT } ![i] = 1]$
 $\land messages' = messages \cup RequestVoteSet(i)$
 $\land \text{UNCHANGED } \langle state, term, vote\_granted,$
 $voted\_for, establish\_leadership \rangle$

$KeepAliveSet(i) \triangleq \{$
 $[fSrc \mapsto i, fDst \mapsto s, fType \mapsto \text{``AppendEntryReq''}, fTerm \mapsto term[i]]$
  $: s \in Servers \setminus \{i\}$
$\}$

$Leader(i) \triangleq$
 $\land state[i] = \text{``Leader''}$
 $\land establish\_leadership[i] = 0$
 $\land establish\_leadership' = [establish\_leadership \text{ EXCEPT } ![i] = 1]$
 $\land messages' = messages \cup KeepAliveSet(i)$
 $\land \text{UNCHANGED } \langle state, voted\_for, term, vote\_granted, vote\_requested \rangle$

9.3.5   Prune Messages with Stale Terms

When a node's term advances, all messages targeted to this node with older terms are discarded. Keeping messages with stale terms allows the model checker to verify the node correctly discards them, but can exponentially grow the state machine. To simplify the model, we can prune stale messages as we add a new message:

$AddMessage(to\_add,\ msgs)\ \triangleq$
> LET
>> $pruned \triangleq \{msg \in msgs :$
>> $\neg(msg.fDst = to\_add.fDst \wedge msg.fTerm < to\_add.fTerm)\}$
> IN
>> $pruned \cup \{to\_add\}$

$RemoveMessage(to\_remove,\ msgs)\ \triangleq$

9.4   Safety

One of the goals of the protocol is to ensure the cluster only has one leader. The clusters can have multiple leaders due to unfavorable network connections. For example, a leader node is partitioned off and a new leader is elected. However, even when the cluster has multiple leaders, they *must* be on different terms. The leader with the highest term is effectively the *true leader*. This invariant can be implemented like so:

$LeaderUniqueTerm \triangleq$
> $\forall s1,\ s2 \in Servers :$
> $(\wedge\ state[s1] = \text{"Leader"}$
> $\wedge\ state[s2] = \text{"Leader"}$
> $\wedge\ s1 \neq s2)$
> $\Rightarrow (term[s1] \neq term[s2])$

For every pair of nodes, they cannot both be Leaders and have the same term.

9.5   Liveness

In any failure recovery scenario, the nodes in the cluster converge to a higher term value either voluntarily or involuntarily. For example:

- A node timed out and started a new election on a new term

- A partitioned follower receives a heartbeat from a new leader on a new term

- A candidate receiving a request vote from another candidate on a higher term

In any case, a node's term number always increases. This can be described as below:

$$Converge \triangleq$$
$$\forall s \in Servers :$$
$$term[s] = 0 \rightsquigarrow term[s] = MaxTerm - MaxDiff$$

Instead of *MaxTerm*, we use *MaxTerm-MaxDiff* to ensure the liveness property is always upheld even after *Normalization*. However, running *Spec* against TLC now will encounter a set of stuttering issues. We also need to update the fairness description to ensure all possible actions are called when the enabling conditions are *eventually always* true:

$$Liveness \triangleq$$
$$\land \forall i \in Servers :$$
$$\land \text{WF}_{vars}(Leader(i))$$
$$\land \text{WF}_{vars}(Candidate(i))$$
$$\land \text{WF}_{vars}(Follower(i))$$
$$\land \text{WF}_{vars}(\exists\, msg \in messages : Receive(msg))$$

Part III

Examples with PlusCal

PlusCal is a C-like syntax that allows designer to describe their specification using a pseudo programming language. An use case for PlusCal is to specify lockless or wait-free data structures.

It is possible to express concurrent data structures in TLA+ native notation. To express a function that can be concurrently executed, the specification needs to use a PC-like variable to track the statement a context is currently executing. This is fairly tedious (and possibly error-prone), making PlusCal a more organic tool to express these designs.

Chapter 10

SPSC Lockless Queue

A single producer single consumer (SPSC) lockless queue is a data exchange queue between a producer and a consumer. The SPSC lockless queue enables data exchange between producer and consumer without the use of a lock, allowing both producer and consumer to make progress in all scenarios.

An example application of an SPSC queue is a data exchange interface between the ASIC and the CPU in a driver implementation.

A real implementation needs to account for memory ordering effects specific to the architecture. For example, ARM has a weak memory ordering model where read/write may appear out-of-order between CPUs. In this chapter, we will assume *logical* execution order where each command is perceived as issued sequentially (even across CPUs) to focus the discussion on describing the system using TLA+.

10.1 Design

The following describes the SPSC queue requirements:

- Two executing context, reader and writer
- Writer pointer advances after write

89

- Reader pointer advances after reading

- If read pointer equals write pointer, queue is empty

- If writer pointer + 1 equals read pointer, queue is full

The following is an example of an SPSC queue:

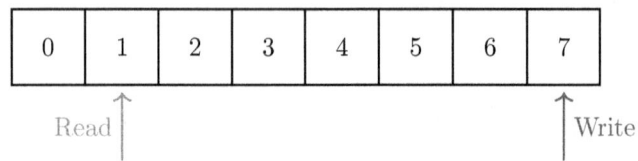

Since the reader and writer execute in different contexts, the instructions in a read and write can interleave in *any* way imaginable:

- Reader empty check can happen just as the writer is writing data

- Writer full check can happen just as the reader is reading data

- Reading and writing can occur concurrently

The key observation is the index held by the write pointer is reserved by the writer. Similarly, the index held by the read pointer is reserved by the reader. The only exception is when the read pointer equals to write pointer, then the queue is empty. Given the possible ways the reader and writer execution can interleave, we can use TLA+ to verify the design.

10.2 Specification

The following is a snippet of the specification written in PlusCal:

```
procedure reader()
begin
r_chk_empty:
        if rptr = wptr then
        r_early_ret:
                return;
```

end if ;
r_read_buf:
    assert $buffer[rptr] \neq 0$;
r_cs:
      $buffer[rptr] := 0$;
r_upd_rtpr:
      $rptr := (rptr + 1)\%N$;
      return ;
end procedure ;

The reader checks if the queue is empty by comparing the read and write pointers. If the queue is empty, reader early returns. If the queue is not empty, the reader reads the index and advances the read pointer.

procedure $writer()$
begin
w_chk_full:
    if $(wptr + 1)\%N = rptr$ **then**
    w_early_ret:
        return ;
    end if ;
w_write_buf:
    assert $buffer[wptr] = 0$;
w_cs:
      $buffer[wptr] := wptr + 1000$;
w_upd_wptr:
      $wptr := (wptr + 1)\%N$;
      return ;
end procedure ;

The writer checks if the queue is full checking if there's more space to write to. If the queue is full, the writer early exists. If the queue is not full, a writer writes to the queue and advances the write pointer.

The key insight here is the read and write pointer effectively *reserves* the index they are pointing to. The state of the indices is unknown to the other context. Assume a reader index of k, the writer cannot write to index k since the reader might be reading from it. The only time a writer can write to k is when the read index is no longer k, suggesting the reader is done with the index. Symmetrically reasoning applies with the write index.

10.3   Safety

A correctness property for a lockless algorithm is to ensure reader and writer cannot access the same index at the same time. Both reader and writer can be working inside their critical section, but they *cannot* be working on the same index. The following formula describes this safety property:

$MutualExclusion \triangleq$
$\qquad \neg((pc[WRITER] = \text{``w\_cs''})$
$\qquad \wedge (pc[READER] = \text{``r\_cs''})$
$\qquad \wedge rptr = wptr)$

10.4   Liveness

For liveness, we want to check the queue never hangs. This can be described as all indices are eventually used and unused:

$Liveness \triangleq$
$\qquad \wedge \forall k \in 0 \mathrel{..} N - 1 :$
$\qquad buffer[k] \neq 0 \rightsquigarrow buffer[k] = 0$
$\qquad \wedge \forall k \in 0 \mathrel{..} N - 1 :$
$\qquad buffer[k] = 0 \rightsquigarrow buffer[k] \neq 0$

Chapter 11

SPMC Lockless Queue

As the name suggests, an SPMC lockless queue supports a single producer *multiple* consumer usage topology.

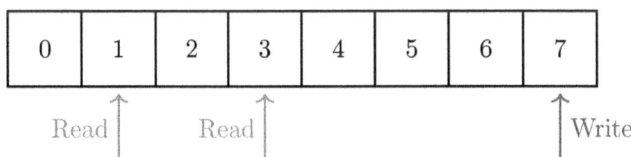

An SPMC queue can be tricky to get right. There are many things to consider:

- Readers can lapse each other.

- Readers can compete for reading indices.

- Readers can lapse writer.

- One reader can starve other readers.

- A slow reader can block the system.

And under all circumstances, system *correctness* must be maintained.

11.1 Design

For the design:

- SPMC is implemented as a circular queue with the size of N

- The status of the individual index is represented as a status array of size N

- The status of each index is either *UNUSED*, *WRITTEN*, or *READING*

- Each reader maintains its own read pointer

- A *outstanding* counter is incremented by the writer when the write is complete, and decremented by the reader when it reserves a read

Whenever the write finishes a write, it increments *outstanding* to indicate some buffer is ready to read.

To read, a reader performs a two-step reservation:

- The reader decrements *outstanding*. A successful decrement means the reader is *guaranteed* a read index.

- After successful decrement of *outstanding*, the reader walks its read pointer until it successfully reserves the next available index to read. This is done by attempting to CAS update an index from *WRITTEN* to *READING*. If the update fails, then the index was already reserved by another reader.

There may be more than one approach to implementing SPMC, the above description is what we will implement in this chapter.

11.2 Specification

The following is the core reader implementation:

procedure *reader*( )
variable

$i = self$;
begin
r_chk_empty:
   if $outstanding \neq 0$ **then**
    $outstanding := outstanding - 1$;
   else
    r_early_ret:
      return ;
   end if ;
r_try_lock:
   if $status[rptr[i]] = WRITTEN$ **then**
    $status[rptr[i]] := READING$;
   else
    r_retry:
      $rptr[i] := (rptr[i] + 1)\%N$;
      goto r_try_lock ;
   end if ;
r_data_chk:
   assert $buffer[rptr[i]] = rptr[i] + 1000$;
r_read_buf:
   $buffer[rptr[i]] := 0$;
r_unlock:
   $status[rptr[i]] := UNUSED$;
r_done:
   return ;
end procedure ;

The reader performs a non-zero check on outstanding. If the outstanding is zero, the queue is empty, and the reader early returns.

If outstanding is K, then at most K readers can reserve an index to read. If the system has M readers, then M-K readers will fail to reserve a read index. The readers now compete to reserve a read. More specifically:

- Reader loads outstanding, and stores that onto the local variable counter.

- Reader early returns if the counter is zero

- Reader attempts to update outstanding with CAS using counter and counter - 1.

- If CAS fails, go back to the top and retry.

If non-success is returned, another reader has *won* the reservation. The current reader can attempt to reserve again if *outstanding* is non-zero.

If success is returned, the reader is *guaranteed* a read. However, readers may still compete during index reservation. To reserve an index, a reader issues CAS to update the index status from *WRITTEN* to *READING*. CAS failure indicates another reader has already reserved this index. The reader will bump the read pointer and try to reserve the next index.

Now let us take a look at the writer implementation:

procedure *writer*( ) **begin**
w_chk_full:
    if *outstanding* $= N - 1$ **then**
    w_early_ret:
        return ;
    end if ;
w_chk_st:
    if *status*[*wptr*] $\neq$ *UNUSED* **then**
    w_early_ret2:
        return ;
    end if ;
w_write_buf:
    buffer[*wptr*] $:=$ *wptr* $+ 1000$;
w_mark_written:
    status[*wptr*] $:=$ *WRITTEN* ;
w_inc_wptr:
    wptr $:= (wptr + 1)\%N$;
w_inc:
    outstanding $:=$ *outstanding* $+ 1$;
w_done:

return;
end procedure ;

The writer first checks outstanding, and early returns if the queue is full. After the fullness check, the writer then checks if the current index is UNUSED. This is to account for the edge case where a reader has performed the reservation first step to decrement outstanding but hasn't done the actual read. If both checks pass, then the writer now has an *UNUSED* index it can write to.

11.3   Safety

When a reader reserves an index to read, the reader must have exclusive access. This can be described as: For any pair of readers inside the critical section, they must operate on different indices:

$ExclusiveReservation \triangleq$
$\quad \forall\, x,\, y \in READERS :$
$\quad (\wedge\, x \neq y$
$\quad \wedge\, pc[x] = \text{``r\_read\_buf''}$
$\quad \wedge\, pc[y] = \text{``r\_read\_buf''})$
$\quad \Rightarrow (rptr[x] \neq rptr[y])$

Similarly, for any reader and writer inside the critical section, must operate on different indices as well:

$ExclusiveReadWrite \triangleq$
$\quad \forall\, x \in READERS :$
$\quad (\wedge\, pc[x] = \text{``r\_read\_buf''}$
$\quad \wedge\, pc[WRITER] = \text{``w\_write\_buf''})$
$\quad \Rightarrow (rptr[x] \neq wptr)$

11.4   Liveness

All indices must be used as the system runs. The following verifies all unused indices are eventually used, and all used indices are eventually unused:

$Liveness \triangleq$
$\quad \land \forall k \in 0 .. N - 1 :$
$\quad buffer[k] = 0 \rightsquigarrow buffer[k] \neq 0$
$\quad \land \forall k \in 0 .. N - 1 :$
$\quad buffer[k] \neq 0 \rightsquigarrow buffer[k] = 0$

The following describes a more subtle scenario. We need to ensure the system remains functional even if readers complete out-of-order. The following describes such a scenario, where two non-contiguous indices have been reserved for reading. In this case, we expect the indices to eventually be re-used. This means the the system remains functional after such scenario.

$Liveness2 \triangleq$
$\quad \forall k \in 0 .. N - 3 :$
$\quad \land (\land status[k] = READING$
$\quad \land status[k + 1] = UNUSED$
$\quad \land status[k + 2] = READING)$
$\quad \rightsquigarrow (status[k] = WRITTEN)$
$\quad \land (\land status[k] = READING$
$\quad \land status[k + 1] = UNUSED$
$\quad \land status[k + 2] = READING)$
$\quad \rightsquigarrow (status[k + 2] = WRITTEN)$

Part IV

System Modeling

Specifications described so far have been designed to with finite state space to allow model checker to explore all states and prove correctness. In this section, we will relax this and allow infinite state space.

This uses TLA+ as a *prototyping* tool. By definition, the model checker cannot verify infinite sate space. However, for all states it does explore, it will verify safety properties and highlight all the violations. This enables designer to quickly iterate on design to flesh out what may or may not work. Per 80/20 rule, the model checker will very quickly identify obvious violations in the design.

Once settled on a design and model checker no longer reports violation in any practical amount of time, one can always simplify the specification into finite space to exhaustively prove correctness.

Chapter 12

KV Store with Cache

LRU cache, or least-recently-used cache, is a finite-sized cache that evicts the least-recently-used entry when full. Modern CPU architecture supports multi-layer cache. Caches closer to the CPU are faster, but also smaller. Cache is designed to take advantage of temporal locality, where recently accessed data isgenerally likely to be re-accessed in near future.

Caches are also applied more broadly: CDNs (content delivery networks) are a group of geographically distributed servers close to users in different parts of the world. Redis is a high-performance in-memory key-value store, effectively a cache layer without underlying storage. The list of examples goes on and on.

12.1   Design

In this chapter, we will describe a simple key-value store with a fixed-sized write-back LRU cache. The size of the key-value store is assumed unbounded. LRU cache acts as a fast access buffer until it's full. When it's full, the least-recently-used entry key-value pair is evicted into the main memory.

Similar to a system with a cache, a key may exist in both the cache

and memory with different values. The key-value pair in the cache is
assumed up-to-date, while the key-value pair in memory may be stale.
When the key-value pair is evicted from the cache, the key in memory
is synchronized by write-back from the cache.

We will implement three specifications in this chapter: LRU cache,
KV store, and Test, with one building on another. The KV store is
implemented using the LRU cache, and Test verifies the KV stores.

12.2   LRU Cache

LRU cache can be implemented using three data structures:

- Linked list to track key access recency

- Lookup table to track key and recency list iterator

- Lookup table to track the key-value pair

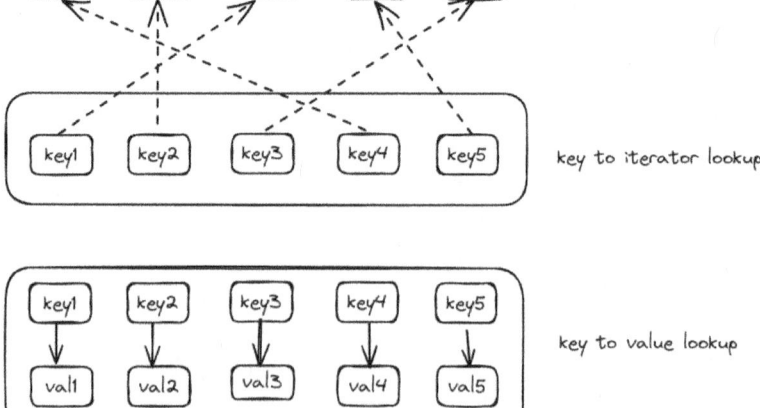

Recency list is a doubly-linked list where the most recently accessed item is at the tail. On read or write of an existing key, the key
to iterator lookup table is used to identify the key to update. The

identified key is then moved to the tail of the recency list to indicate recent access. Finally, the key-value table is updated if needed. When inserting a new key-value pair, the head of the recency list is evicted to make space, if required.

When specifying the LRU cache with TLA+, we can omit the key to iterator table to simplify the specification. Recency list can be implemented as a *tuple*, and a key-value table as a *function*.

12.2.1 Specification

The following implements the LRU put function:

$Put(k,\ v) \triangleq$
IF $k \in$ DOMAIN lru_kv THEN
  replace
  $\wedge\ lru\_recency' = Append(SelectSeq(\ lru\_recency,$ LAMBDA $x : x \neq k),\ k)$
  $\wedge\ lru\_kv' = [n \in$ DOMAIN $lru\_kv \mapsto$ IF $n = k$ THEN v ELSE $lru\_kv[n]]$
  $\wedge$ UNCHANGED lru_size
ELSE
  IF $Len(lru\_recency) \neq lru\_size$ THEN
    add
    $\wedge\ lru\_recency' = Append(lru\_recency,\ k)$
    $\wedge\ lru\_kv' = [n \in$ DOMAIN $lru\_kv \cup \{k\} \mapsto n]$
    $\wedge$ UNCHANGED lru_size
  ELSE
    replace oldest
    $\wedge\ lru\_recency' = Append(SelectSeq(\ lru\_recency,$
    LAMBDA $x : x \neq lru\_recency[1]),\ k)$
    $\wedge\ lru\_kv' = [n \in ($DOMAIN $lru\_kv \cup \{k\}) \setminus \{lru\_recency[1]\} \mapsto$
    IF $n \neq k$ THEN $lru\_kv[n]$ ELSE $v]$
    $\wedge$ UNCHANGED lru_size

When the implementation needs to extract a key and move it to the end, it uses *SelectSeq* to remove the targeted key and *Append* to append the key to the end. When updating lru_kv, the keyspace is expanded with k. In the case keyspace is full, then *lru_recency[1]* (least recent entry in LRU) is evicted.

12.2.2 Safety

For safety, we want to ensure values in *lru_recency* match with keys in *lru_function*. Similarly, LRU size cannot exceed *lru_size*.

> $Consistent \triangleq$
> $\quad \land \{lru\_recency[k] : k \in \text{DOMAIN } lru\_recency\} = \text{DOMAIN } lru\_kv$
> $\quad \land Cardinality(\text{DOMAIN } lru\_kv) \leq lru\_size$

12.2.3 Liveness

Omitted from this chapter.

12.3 KV Store

The KV store itself is pretty straightforward in design. Naively we need a single *function* to implement a table that holds the key-value pairs. The slight complexity is integrating LRU into the KV store. This is described in the *Update* function:

$Update(k, v) \triangleq$
$\quad$ IF $LRU!Contains(k)$ THEN
$\quad\quad \land LRU!Put(k, v)$
$\quad\quad \land$ UNCHANGED kv
$\quad\quad \land latency' = CACHED$
$\quad$ ELSE $\quad$ LRU does not contain k
$\quad\quad \land$ IF $LRU!IsFull$ THEN
$\quad\quad\quad$ LET
$\quad\quad\quad\quad pair \triangleq LRU!GetLeastRecent$
$\quad\quad\quad\quad key \triangleq$ CHOOSE $only \in$ DOMAIN $pair$: TRUE
$\quad\quad\quad\quad value \triangleq pair[key]$
$\quad\quad\quad$ IN
$\quad\quad\quad\quad$ Evicted from LRU and write to memory
$\quad\quad\quad\quad \land kv' = [x \in$ DOMAIN $kv \cup \{ key\} \mapsto$

$\text{IF } x = key \text{ THEN } value \text{ ELSE } kv[x]]$
ELSE
   UNCHANGED kv
$\wedge LRU!Put(k,\, v)$
$\wedge latency' = EVICT$

If the LRU contains the key (full or not), we simply update the LRU. The LRU will update its internal recency list. If LRU doesn't contain the key, we have two possible scenarios. If the LRU is not full, we can simply insert it into the LRU. If the LRU is full, we need to evict the least recently used key-value pair write back to KV store, and insert the new key-value pair into the LRU.

12.3.1 Safety

Omitted from this chapter.

12.3.2 Liveness

Omitted from this chapter.

12.4 Test

Putting everything together, we want to characterize the design and confirm wget get the expected latency improvement.

12.4.1 Spec

The core of the test is pretty straightforward, we assume the usual 80/20 rule where 80% of the traffic are cache hits and 20% are cache misses. This can be simulated using the existential qualifier:

$Next \triangleq$
   $\vee \, \exists \, p \in 1 \mathinner{\ldotp\ldotp} 10 :$
   $\wedge \text{ IF } p > 2 \text{ THEN}$
      cached
      $\wedge \, \exists \, k \in \text{DOMAIN } lru\_kv :$

$\wedge KV ! Update(k, \ lru\_kv[k])$
$\wedge written' = [x \in \text{DOMAIN } written \setminus \{k\} \mapsto$
IF $x = k$ THEN k ELSE $written[x]]$
ELSE
    cache miss
    / PrintT(p)
    $\wedge \exists k \in DataSet \setminus \text{DOMAIN } \ lru\_kv :$
    $\wedge KV ! Update(k, \ k)$
    $\wedge written' = [x \in \text{DOMAIN } written \setminus \{k\} \mapsto$
    IF $x = k$ THEN k ELSE $written[x]]$

12.4.2   Safety

We want to verify the KV store with cache returns the correct value for all the key-value pairs written:

$Consistent \ \triangleq$
    $\forall k \in \text{DOMAIN } written :$
    $KV ! Read(k) = written[k]$

12.4.3   Liveness

Omitted for this chapter.

12.5   Statistical Sampling

To collect statistical latency numbers for the design, include the Community Module CSV and define Safety property:

$CSVFile \ \triangleq$
    "stat.csv"

$Stats \ \triangleq$
    $\wedge CSVWrite("\%1\$s", \langle latency \rangle, CSVFile)$

The Safety property $Stats$ will be triggered in every state, collecting the latency number in a .csv. To generate the .csv:

```
rm -rf *.csv
    && java -cp tla2tools.jar tlc2.TLC \
        -generate -note ~/dev/tla/tla/test_kv
```

The latency numbers have now been collected into stat.csv. Now let us count the latency numbers:

```
cat stat.csv  | grep 10 -ws | wc
    && cat stat.csv  | grep 100 -ws | wc

  34674    34674   104022
   9239     9239    36956
```

With a total of 43913 samples, cache hit happens about 78.9% of the time. This closely matches the desired 80% cache hit defined in the test.

Chapter 13

Dropbox

In this chapter, we will specify a Dropbox-like service with TLA+ and use the model checker to flesh out the design.

13.1 Design

The simplified Dropbox-like service includes a block server containing all versions of files and a meta server containing metadata for all versions of files. A client maintains its copy of all the file metadata (possibly stale) and selectively downloads the physical files as needed to save bandwidth.

Once a client downloads a file, it can make local changes. The modified file can be uploaded if no other clients have uploaded a more recent version. Uploading the file also updates its metadata, which is propagated to all other clients. If multiple clients make changes to the same file, the first one to upload wins and the other clients need to rebase their changes on top of the latest before uploading again.

A nuanced part of the design is client synchronization with the remote is not deterministic. The client can work offline for an extended period and make changes to a file when other clients upload new versions of the same or other files. The system design needs to account for conflict resolution.

The system design is visualized below:

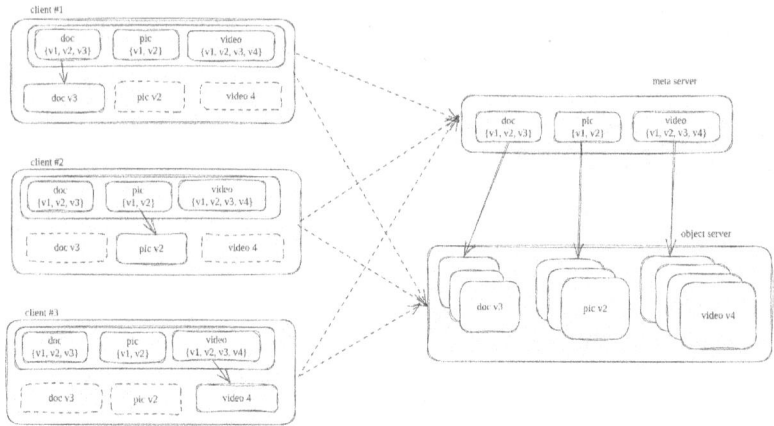

13.2   Spec

The following describes the variables used track system state:

$Init \stackrel{\Delta}{=}$
    $\wedge$ *meta_server* $= [f \in Files \mapsto \{1\}]$
    $\wedge$ *block_server* $= [f \in Files \mapsto \langle 5 \rangle]$
    $\wedge$ *client_meta* $= [k \in Clients \mapsto meta\_server]$
    $\wedge$ *client_change* $= [k \in Clients \mapsto [f \in Files \mapsto \text{FALSE}]]$
    $\wedge$ *client_block* $= [k \in Clients \mapsto \langle \rangle]$

- *meta_server* is a lookup table of filename to a set of revisions.

- *block_server* is a lookup table of filename to a list of sizes, ordered by revision.

- *client_meta* represents the client's local copy of the file meta.

- *client_block* is the client's block storage, only holding a version of the file specified by the client meta.

- *client_change* is a per client per file lookup tracking if the file has been changed locally.

To paint a more concrete picture, this is a snapshot of a state:

```
State 94375:
/\ client_block = [c0 |-> [f0 |-> 9, f1 |-> 5],
                   c1 |-> [f0 |-> 9]]
/\ client_meta = [c0 |-> [f0 |-> 4, f1 |-> 2],
                  c1 |-> [f0 |-> 2, f1 |-> 1]]
/\ block_server = [f0 |-> <<5, 5, 7>>, f1 |-> <<5, 5>>]
/\ meta_server = [f0 |-> 3, f1 |-> 2]
/\ client_change = [c0 |-> [f0 |-> TRUE, f1 |-> FALSE],
                    c1 |-> [f0 |-> TRUE, f1 |-> FALSE]]
```

In this state:

- The meta and block server have 2 files: File 0 has 3 revisions and File 1 has 2.

- Client 0 downloaded both files 0 and 1.

- Client 0 modified file 0 (bumped the revision to 4) but did not modify file 1.

- Client 1 metadata is stale for both Files 0 and 1, but modified file 0.

- Client 1 has downloaded the older revision of file 1 and modified it.

The set of actions allowed is defined below:

$Next \triangleq$
$\quad \vee \exists k \in Clients :$
$\quad \exists f \in Files :$
$\quad \vee SyncMeta(k, f)$
$\quad \vee Download(k, f)$

$\lor$ *Modify*(k, f)
$\lor$ *Upload*(k, f)

In every state, the system can choose to synchronize the metadata of a file, download a file, modify a file, or upload a changed file. Some of these operations depend on each other. For example, a file can only be modified if it is downloaded.

Let us first take a look at *SyncMeta*:

TailIndex$(s) \triangleq$
　MaxS(DOMAIN s)

SyncObject$(k, f) \triangleq$
　IF $f \in$ DOMAIN *client_block*$[k]$ THEN
　　client_block$'$
　　　$= [$*client_block* EXCEPT $![k]$
　　　　$= [$*client_block*$[k]$ EXCEPT $![f]$
　　　　　$=$ *block_server*$[f][$*TailIndex*(*block_server*$[f]$)$]]]$
　　ELSE
　　　UNCHANGED *client_block*

SyncMeta$(k, f) \triangleq$
　IF *client_meta*$[k][f] <$ *meta_server*$[f]$
　　$\lor$ (*client_meta*$[k][f] =$ *meta_server*$[f] \land$ *client_change*$[k][f]$) THEN
　　sync client meta
　　$\land$ *client_meta*$'$
　　　$= [$*client_meta* EXCEPT $![k]$
　　　　$= [$*client_meta*$[k]$ EXCEPT $![f]$
　　　　　$=$ *meta_server*$[f]]]]$
　　sync downloaded file
　　$\land$ *SyncObject*(k, f)
　　$\land$ *client_change*$'$
　　　$= [$*client_change* EXCEPT $![k]$
　　　　$= [$*client_change*$[k]$ EXCEPT $![f] =$ FALSE$]]$
　　$\land$ UNCHANGED $\langle$*meta_server*, *block_server*$\rangle$
　　ELSE

$\wedge$ UNCHANGED *vars*

The client syncs with the remote when it is out-of-date. This happens when: the remote has a higher revision of the file, or if the client has the same revision of the file but *local_change* is set. The current implementation discards and forces updates to remote. Practically, the client should rebase and resolve the conflict.

SyncObject resets the file to match the remote. This is done by getting the size of the latest revision for the file. TLA+ doesn't natively provide a function to get the last element, so *TailIndex* function was added to facilitate this.

The following defines *Download*:

$Download(k, f) \triangleq$
       only download if meta is up-to-date with no local changes
    $\wedge\ client\_change[k][f] =$ FALSE
    $\wedge\ client\_meta[k][f] = meta\_server[f]$
    Download the latest version
    $\wedge\ client\_block'$
      $= [client\_block$ EXCEPT $![k]$
      $= [ff \in$ DOMAIN $client\_block[k] \cup \{f\}$
        $\mapsto$ IF $ff \neq f$
      THEN $client\_block[k][ff]$
      ELSE $block\_server[f][MaxS($DOMAIN $block\_server[f])]]]$
    $\wedge$ UNCHANGED $\langle client\_change,\ client\_meta,\ meta\_server,\ block\_server\rangle$

The client only downloads if the file meta is up-to-date and has not been modified locally.

The *Modify* function is defined below:

$Modify(k, f) \triangleq$
    $\wedge\ client\_change[k][f] =$ FALSE
    add new version to client meta
    $\wedge\ client\_meta'$
      $= [client\_meta$ EXCEPT $![k]$

$$= [client\_meta[k] \text{ EXCEPT } ![f]$$
$$= client\_meta[k][f] + 1]]$$
bump client block
$$\land f \in \text{DOMAIN } client\_block[k]$$
$$\land \exists s \in Sizes :$$
$$client\_block'$$
$$= [client\_block \text{ EXCEPT } ![k]$$
$$= [client\_block[k] \text{ EXCEPT } ![f] = s]]$$
$$\land client\_change'$$
$$= [client\_change \text{ EXCEPT } ![k]$$
$$= [client\_change[k] \text{ EXCEPT } ![f] = \text{TRUE}]]$$
$$\land \text{UNCHANGED } \langle meta\_server, block\_server \rangle$$

A file can only be modified if it hasn't been. While the client can modify a file multiple times, this is modeled as a single revision until the file is uploaded to remote. A new version of the file is created by bumping the client's local file meta, marking the file as changed, and assigning the file a random size usingan existential qualifier.

Finally, let's take a look at *Upload*:

$$Upload(k, f) \triangleq$$
client is ahead of the remote with local change
$$\land meta\_server[f] < client\_meta[k][f]$$
$$\land client\_change[k][f]$$
$$\land meta\_server'$$
$$= [meta\_server \text{ EXCEPT } ![f]$$
$$= client\_meta[k][f]] \text{ upload our version}$$
$$\land block\_server' = [block\_server \text{ EXCEPT } ![f]$$
$$= Append(block\_server[f], client\_block[k][f])]$$
$$\land client\_change'$$
$$= [client\_change \text{ EXCEPT } ![k]$$
$$= [client\_change[k] \text{ EXCEPT } ![f] = \text{FALSE}]]$$
$$\land \text{UNCHANGED } \langle client\_block, client\_meta \rangle$$

Client uploads when it is ahead of remote and has local changes. If the client is not ahead of the remote, the remote may have a newer version of the file. In such a case, the client will call *SyncMeta* to synchronize the remote.

13.3   Safety

Unmodified files on the client must match their remote counterpart. This can be verified by comparing the sizes. Note that the client may have a partial set of files locally, so the property is only verified if the file exists on the client:

$Consistent \triangleq$
$\quad \forall\, k \in Clients:$
$\quad \forall\, f \in Files:$
$\quad\quad (client\_change[k][f] = \text{FALSE} \wedge f \in \text{DOMAIN } client\_block[k])$
$\quad\quad\quad \Rightarrow client\_block[k][f] = block\_server[f][client\_meta[k][f]]$

The client can make local changes to the file, but all changes are contained in a single revision until the file is uploaded. The client can be offline for an extended period while remote revision increases. In any case, the client's file revision number can be far behind, but at most one ahead:

$Consistent2 \triangleq$
$\quad \forall\, k \in Clients:$
$\quad \forall\, f \in Files:$
$\quad\quad f \in \text{DOMAIN } client\_meta[k]$
$\quad\quad\quad \Rightarrow (client\_meta[k][f] - meta\_server[f]) \leq 1$

When the client modifies a file, the file revision is bumped. In such a case the client has been offline for an extended amount of time, and the remote file revision may be far ahead. If the client's file revision is ahead of remote, the file *must* have been modified:

$Consistent3 \triangleq$
$\quad \forall\, k \in Clients:$
$\quad \forall\, f \in Files:$
$\quad\quad client\_meta[k][f] > meta\_server[f] \Rightarrow client\_change[k][f]$

13.4 Liveness

Omitted for this chapter.

Chapter 14

Decentralized Database

In the era of big data today, localized instances of relational databases is no longer enough to hold the volume of data for today's requirements. Distributed key-value stores have been of a key area of interest in the past few decades. Offering such as DynamoDB, Cassandra, and Azure Cloud are a few examples of what industry leaders are offering to address the data problem.

A cluster of nodes collectively offers service provided by a distributed key-value store. The nodes independently restart, update, crash, join, or leave the cluster, while the service remains uninterrupted (though with possibly reduced service). As the user base scales, the service must scale accordingly.

Two of the key design principles in distributed data are partition and replication.

A replica group (RG) is a group of nodes that maintain the same set of data. Nodes in an RG often span multiple availability zones (AZ) to maximize uptime. In case of a regional value that wipes out an entire AZ, the other nodes in the RG can still maintain the service albeit at reduced QoS. The nodes in the RG are kept in sync using consensus protocols such as Raft. A write is only completed once it has been recorded by the majority of nodes in the RG.

Partition is a way to split the key space into slices. When the key space is partitioned, an RG is only responsible for a slice of the key space. Bandwidth demand is also amortized across all RGs. Partition is typically done using consistent hashing. Different from traditional hashing, consistent hashing minimizes data movement when nodes join and leave the clusters. Consistent hashing will be covered in detail in a later part of the chapter.

Some of the early distributed database design requires a centralized server for meta management (eg. ZooKeeper). In this chapter, we will specify a fully decentralized key-value store. To simplify the specification, we will assume each node itself is a functioning RG with associated reliability property (this is considered a solved problem with Raft). This chapter will focus on system behavior correctness as RGs join or leave the cluster and associated data migration.

14.1   Consistent Hashing

Before we dive into design details, we must first describe consistent hashing. With a traditional hashing algorithm, changing the size of the hash space requires data movement of the entire cluster. This is very undesirable. Consistent hashing was introduced to minimize data movement, where movement is only required when adding or removing nodes in the affected range.

In consistent hashing, the hash space is assumed to be a ring, where the largest hash value plus one wraps around to the hash of 0. Servers in a consistent hashing cluster take up different ranges in the ring. For a given request, the client where the request lands by hashing the request first, then walks the ring clockwise until it finds a server.

Assume the following example:

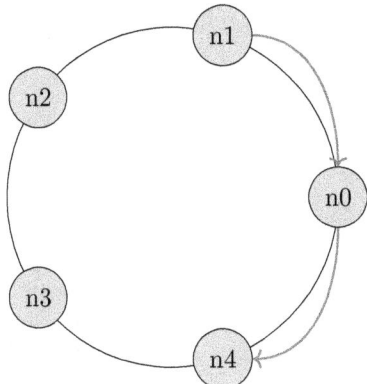

If the request lands between n1 (exclusive) and n0 (inclusive), the request will be processed by n0. Similarly, if the request lands between n0 (exclusive) and n4 (inclusive), the request is to be processed by n4.

Assume a case where n4 goes offline:

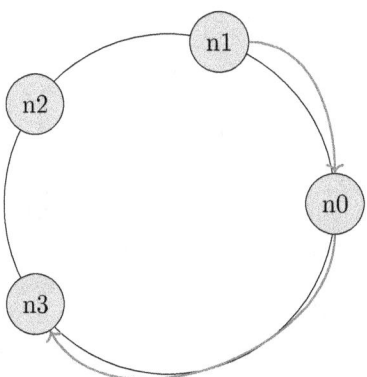

In such a case, requests previously processed by n4 will land on n3 instead. Similarly, if a new node n5 is added:

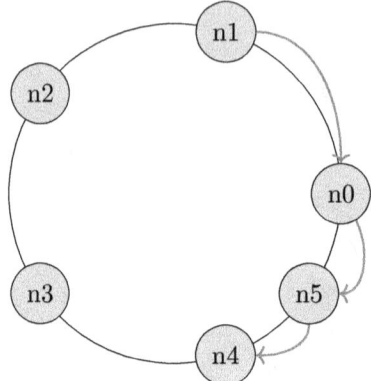

Part of what n4 used to service will now be serviced by n5.

14.2   Gossip Protocol

Without a centralized metadata controller, the nodes learn about their
peers using the gossip protocol. As a new RG enters the cluster, the
design relies on gossip protocol to spread the information. This is a
critical part of the design as will be described later.

14.3   Design

In our design, an RG can be in one of the following states: Offline,
Joining, Online, Leaving. The service starts with a single RG responsible for the entire hash space. Since this is the epoch RG, it directly
transitions into an Online state and can claim any token on the ring.
For simplicity, epoch RG always claims token 0.

The design assumes node failure handling is handled within the
RG, the specification will not model RG crash or restart.

14.3.1   Offline

RG is offline, with no impact on the cluster.

14.3.2   Joining

By definition, the goal of adding an RG U into the cluster is to reduce the load on another RG V. Since RG U is a new member of the cluster, it may not have the latest cluster topology. Once RG U announces its presence via a gossip protocol, it waits for RG V to reach out.

When RG V realizes a new RG can share its burden, RG V will coordinate with RG U to migrate a subset of its data to RG U (the subset RG U will be responsible for). Once data migration is completed: RG U transitions to the Online state and starts servicing requests in its range, while RG V rejects requests to the range RG U has taken over. This range update is also reflected in both RG U and V's local ring cache and communicated during the next round of gossip protocol.

14.3.3   Online

RG is *Online* and responds to and records requests in its hash range.

14.3.4   Leaving

Symmetrically, when an RG U is leaving the cluster, an RG V needs to take over the range and data RG U is currently responsible for. Similarly to join, RG U announced its intent to leave and wait for RG V to reach out and coordinate the handoff.

Note when RG U is still waiting or in the middle of hand-off, it is still *Online* and must respond to request, until RV V fully takes over.

14.4   Specification

Init is defined below:

$offline \triangleq [k \in RGState \mapsto$
IF $k = $ "version" THEN 0
  ELSE IF $k = $ "token" THEN -1
  ELSE IF $k = $ "state" THEN "offline"
  ELSE "unused"]

$seed \triangleq [k \in RGState \mapsto$
  IF $k =$ "version" THEN 1
  ELSE IF $k =$ "token" THEN 0
  ELSE IF $k =$ "state" THEN "online"
  ELSE "unused"$]$
$Init \triangleq$
  $\wedge local\_ring = [i \in RGs \mapsto$
    $[j \in RGs \mapsto$
      IF $i = SeedRG \wedge j = SeedRG$
      THEN $seed$
      ELSE $offline]]$
  $\wedge local\_kv = [i \in RGs \mapsto \{\}]$
  $\wedge debug\_kv = \{\}$
  $\wedge debug = \{\}$

Since RGs operate independently, each RG maintains its view of the ring. This is tracked by $local\_ring$. The cluster is initialized with a single RG $SeedRG$ with $version$ set to 1, $state$ set to online, and claims $token$ 0 on the ring.

$local\_kv$ represents the per RG KV store. $debug\_kv$ records what the client has written, this is used to verify the consistency of the distributed database. Finally, a $debug$ variable is used to hold a token in a failure trace.

The core set of actions permitted by $Spec$ is defined below:

$Next \triangleq$
  $\vee \exists u, v \in RGs :$
  $\wedge Gossip(u, v)$
  $\vee \exists u \in RGs :$
  $\vee Join(u)$
  $\vee JoinMigrate(u)$
  $\vee Leave(u)$
  $\vee LeaveMigrate(u)$
  $\vee \exists u \in RGs :$
  $\wedge \exists k \in KeySpace :$
  $\wedge k \notin debug\_kv$

$$\land\ Write(u,\ k)$$

A RG can *Join* or *Leave* the cluster. However, both are graceful operations requiring coordination of other nodes from the cluster. To completelyjoin or leave, another RG has to either offload or take over the range of thejoining or leaving RG. This is described by *JoinMigrate* and *LeaveMigrate*. Any pair of nodes can *Gossip* to share their understanding of the current cluster state. Finally, a client can *Write* to the database by sending a request to an RG.

Let us take a look at the definition for *Join*:

$ClaimedToken \triangleq$
    LET
        $not\_offline \triangleq \{v \in RGs : local\_ring[v\,][v][\text{"state"}] \neq StateOffline\}$
    IN
        $\{local\_ring[k][k][\text{"token"}] : k \in\ not\_offline\}$

$Join(u) \triangleq$
LET
    $key \triangleq \text{CHOOSE } any \in KeySpace \setminus ClaimedToken : \text{TRUE}$
IN
        Only ever one node joining at a time
    $\land\ local\_ring[u][u][\text{"state"}] =\ StateOffline$
    $\land\ local\_ring' = [local\_ring \text{ EXCEPT }\ ![u]$
      $= [local\_ring[u] \text{ EXCEPT }\ ![u]$
        $= [k \in RGState \mapsto$
        IF $k = \text{"version"}$ THEN $local\_ring[u][u][k\,] + 1$
        ELSE IF $k = \text{"token"}$ THEN key
        ELSE IF $k = \text{"state"}$ THEN $StatePrepare$
        ELSE $\text{"unused"}]]]$
    $\land$ UNCHANGED $\langle local\_kv, debug\_kv,\ debug\rangle$

A RG can only join the cluster if it is currently *Offline*. To join the cluster, the RG must claim an unclaimed token, enter *Joining* state, and announces its intent via *Gossip*.

The design has taken a shortcut to claim an unclaimed token. In a production implementation, a newly joined RG will not know which token is unclaimed. Since the design relies on another RG to *admit* the new RG into the cluster, in the case of a collision the admitting RG can simply ask the RG that wishes to join to pick a different token and restart the process. Practically, the hash space is large enough that collision is unlikely.

The following describes *JoinMigrate*:

RECURSIVE $FindPrevToken(\_,\ \_)$
$FindPrevToken(key,\ ring)\ \triangleq$
    LET
        $condition(v)\ \triangleq\ ring[v][\text{"state"}]\ \neq\ StateOffline$
        $\wedge\ ring[v][\text{"token"}]\ =\ key$
        $exists\ \triangleq\ \exists\,v \in \text{DOMAIN}\ ring : condition\ (v)$
        $owner\ \triangleq\ \text{CHOOSE}\ only \in \text{DOMAIN}\ ring : \ condition(only)$
    IN
        IF $exists$ THEN
        $owner$
        ELSE
           $FindPrevToken((key + N - 1)\ \backslash\ \%N,\ ring)$

$JoinMigrate(u)\ \triangleq$
    LET
        previous token
        $v\ \triangleq\ FindPrevToken((local\_ring[u][u]\ [\text{"token"}] + N - 1)\%N,$
        $local\_ring[u])$
        $all\_keys\ \triangleq\ local\_kv[u]$
        $all\_online\_tokens\ \triangleq\ AllOnlineTokens(u)$
        $v\_token\ \triangleq\ local\_ring[u][v][\text{"token"}]$
        $v\_data\ \triangleq\ DataSet(v\_token,\ all\_online\_tokens\ ,\ all\_keys)$
        $updated\ \triangleq\ [k \in RGState \mapsto$
          IF $k = \text{"version"}$ THEN $local\_ring[u][v]\ [\text{"version"}] + 1$
          ELSE IF $k = \text{"token"}$ THEN $local\_ring[u][\ v][\text{"token"}]$
          ELSE IF $k = \text{"state"}$ THEN $StateOnline$
          ELSE $\text{"unused"}]$
        $merged\ \triangleq\ Merge(u,\ v)$

$$local\_ring\_u \triangleq [merged \text{ EXCEPT } ![u]$$
$$= [merged[u] \text{ EXCEPT } ![v] = updated]]$$
$$local\_ring\_uv \triangleq [local\_ring\_u \text{ EXCEPT } ![\ v]$$
$$= [local\_ring\_u[v] \text{ EXCEPT } ![v] = \ updated]]$$

IN

$\wedge\ Cardinality(AllTokens(u)) \geq 2$
$\wedge\ local\_ring[u][u][\text{"state"}] = \ StateOnline$
$\wedge\ local\_ring[u][v][\text{"state"}] = \ StatePrepare$
$\wedge\ Cardinality(all\_keys) \neq 0$
$\wedge$ IF $v\_data \neq \{\}$ THEN
$\quad \wedge\ local\_ring' = local\_ring\_uv$
$\quad \wedge\ local\_kv' = [k \in RGs \mapsto$
$\quad$ IF $k = u$ THEN $local\_kv[k] \setminus\ v\_data$
$\quad$ ELSE IF $k = v$ THEN $local\_kv[k] \cup\ v\_data$
$\quad$ ELSE $\ local\_kv[k]]$
$\quad$ ELSE
$\qquad$ UNCHANGED $\langle local\_ring, local\_kv \rangle$
$\wedge$ UNCHANGED $\langle debug\_kv, debug \rangle$

A RG U walks its local ring counter-clockwise to find the first neighboring RG V. If RG V is in *Joining* state, this allows RG U to offload part of its range to RG V and admit RG V into the cluster. This coordination also includes data migration, since some of the keys RG U has will be owned by RG V as well. At the end of the process, both RG U and V update their local ring cache of each other's state and propagate that in subsequent rounds of *Gossip*.

In a practical implementation, the data migration process might take a while. The RGs maintains merkle-trees for its data and uses that to determine migration status. Once data migration completes, the range switchover is atomic. RG U stops servicing requests to the range RG V has taken over and redirects the requests to RG V either explicitly or implicitly via gossip protocol.

The following defines *Leave*:

$Leave(u) \triangleq$
$\quad$ LET

$updated \triangleq [k \in RGState \mapsto$
 IF $k =$ "version" THEN $local\_ring[u][u][\ k] + 1$
 ELSE IF $k =$ "token" THEN $local\_ring[u]\ [u][k]$
 ELSE IF $k =$ "state" THEN $StateExit$
 ELSE "unused"$]$

IN

 can only leave if we are already online
$\wedge\ local\_ring[u][u]["state"] =\ StateOnline$
 can only leave if there's at least another server to migrate data to
$\wedge\ Cardinality(AllOnlineTokens(u)) \geq 2$
$\wedge\ local\_ring' = [local\_ring$ EXCEPT $![u]$
 $= [local\_ring[u]$ EXCEPT $![u]$
 $= updated]]$
$\wedge$ UNCHANGED $\langle local\_kv,\ debug\_kv,\ debug \rangle$

Similar to *Join*, a RG can leave if it is *Online*, and not the only RG in the cluster.

Correspondingly, the following defines *LeaveMigrate*:

$LeaveMigrate(u) \triangleq$
 LET
  $token \triangleq (local\_ring[u][u]["token"] +\ N - 1)\%N$
  $v \triangleq FindPrevToken(token, local\_ring[u])$
  $data \triangleq local\_kv[u]$

  $updated \triangleq [k \in RGState \mapsto$
   IF $k =$ "version" THEN $local\_ring[u][v]\ ["version"] + 1$
   ELSE IF $k =$ "token" THEN $local\_ring[u][\ v]["token"]$
   ELSE IF $k =$ "state" THEN $StateOffline$
   ELSE "unused"$]$
  $merged \triangleq Merge(u, v)$
  $local\_ring\_u \triangleq [merged$ EXCEPT $![u]$
   $= [merged[u]$ EXCEPT $![v] = updated]]$
  $local\_ring\_uv \triangleq [local\_ring\_u$ EXCEPT $![\ v]$
   $= [local\_ring\_u[v]$ EXCEPT $![v] =\ updated]]$
 IN

  copying from v to u

$\land\ local\_ring[u][u][\text{"state"}]\ =\ StateOnline$

$\land\ local\_ring[u][v][\text{"state"}]\ =\ StateExit$

    update version

$\land\ local\_ring'\ =\ local\_ring\_uv$

    migrate data

$\land\ local\_kv'\ =\ [k\ \in\ RGs\ \mapsto$

IF $k = v$ THEN $\{\}$

ELSE IF $k = u$ THEN $local\_kv[v]\ \cup\ local\_kv[u]$

ELSE $local\_kv[k]]$

$\land$ UNCHANGED $\langle debug\_kv,\ debug \rangle$

Similar to *JoinMigrate*: when RG U finds out its neighbor RV V intends to leave the cluster, it coordinates with RG V to migrate its data and range.

Gossip is defined below:

$Merge(u,\ v)\ \triangleq$

    LET

        $updated(w)\ \triangleq$ IF $local\_ring[u][w]\ [\text{"version"}]$

        $<\ local\_ring[v][w][\text{"version"}]$ THEN

        $local\_ring[v][w]$

        ELSE

            $local\_ring[u][w]$

    IN

        $[k\ \in\ RGs\ \mapsto$ IF $k = u \lor k = v$

        THEN $[w\ \in\ RGs\ \mapsto\ updated(w)]$

        ELSE $local\_ring[k]]$

$Gossip(u,\ v)\ \triangleq$

    $\land\ local\_ring[u][u][\text{"state"}]\ \neq\ StateOffline$

    $\land\ local\_ring[v][v][\text{"state"}]\ \neq\ StateOffline$

    $\land\ local\_ring'\ =\ Merge(u,\ v)$

    $\land$ UNCHANGED $\langle local\_kv,\ debug\_kv,\ debug \rangle$

Gossip can happen between any pair of nodes as long as they are both *not Offline*.

Finally, let us take a look at *Write*:

$Write(u, k) \triangleq$
LET
  $owner \triangleq FindNextToken(k, local\_ring[u])$
IN
   only accept if u is owner
   $\land \lor local\_ring[u][u][\text{"state"}] = StateOnline$
   $\lor local\_ring[u][u][\text{"state"}] = StateExit$
   $\land u = owner$
   $\land local\_kv' = [local\_kv \text{ EXCEPT } ![u]$
   $= local\_kv[u] \cup \{k\}]$
   $\land debug\_kv' = debug\_kv \cup \{k\}$
   $\land \text{UNCHANGED } \langle local\_ring, debug \rangle$

An RG in *Joining* state cannot accept requests because it has not been admitted into the cluster. A RG in *Leaving* state must still accept requests because the hand-off hasn't been completed. The specification enforces an RG to only accept requests in its data range. A practical implementation will include some sort of explicit or implicit redirect.

14.5 Safety

The design assumes RG maintains its own data replication internally. This implies data should not be between RGs:

$DataUnique \triangleq$
 $\forall u, v \in RGs :$
 $\land u \neq v \Rightarrow local\_kv[u] \cap local\_kv[v] = \{\}$

Every RG maintains a set of key values in its KV store. We want to confirm all the keys in the KV store has not been misplaced:

$TokenLocation \triangleq$
 $\forall u \in RGs :$
 $\forall k \in local\_kv[u] :$
 $u = FindNextToken(k, local\_ring[u])$

The union of all the KV stores needs to mirror all the data written:

$KVConsistent \triangleq$
$\quad \land$ UNION $\{local\_kv[n] : n \in RGs\} = debug\_kv$

14.6   Liveness

Omitted for this chapter.

Part V

Reference

Chapter 15

Fairness

For rigorous definition and proof, please refer to [1]. This chapter focus on the application fairness by describing an elevator that eventually makes it to the top floor:

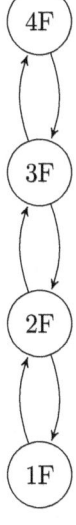

15.1   Liveness

Consider the following elevator *Spec*:

```
────────────────────── MODULE elevator ──────────────────────
EXTENDS Integers
VARIABLES a
vars ≜ ⟨a⟩
TOP       ≜ 4
BOTTOM  ≜ 1
Init ≜
      ∧ a = BOTTOM
Up ≜
      ∧ a ≠ TOP
      ∧ a′ = a + 1
Down ≜
      ∧ a ≠ BOTTOM
      ∧ a′ = a − 1
Spec ≜
      ∧ Init
      ∧ □[Up ∨ Down]ₐ
──────────────────────────────────────────────────────────────
```

The building has a set of floors and the elevator can go either up
or down. The elevator keeps going up until it's the top floor, or keeps
going down until it's the bottom floor. TLC will pass the spec as is.

Let's introduce a liveness property. The elevator should always at
least go to the second floor:

Liveness ≜
    ∧ $a = 1 \rightsquigarrow a = 2$

The model checker will report a violation on this property:

```
Error: Temporal properties were violated.
Error: The following behavior constitutes a counter-example:
State 1: <Initial predicate>
a = 1
```

State 2: Stuttering

Since *Spec* permits *stuttering*, the state machine is allowed to per-petually stay on 1F and *never* go to 2F. This can be fixed by intro-ducing a fairness description.

15.2   Weak Fairness

Weak fairness is defined as:

$$\Diamond\Box(ENABLED\langle A\rangle_v) \Rightarrow \Box\Diamond\langle A\rangle_v \tag{15.1}$$

$ENABLED\langle A\rangle$ represents *conditions required* for action A. The above translates to: if conditions required for action A to occur is *eventually always* true, then action A will *always eventually* happen.

Without weak fairness defined, the elevator may *stutter* at 1F and never go to 2F. Weak fairness states that if the conditions of an action are*eventually always* true (ie. elevator decides to stay on 1F but *can* go up), the elevator *always eventually* goes up.

$Spec \triangleq$
  $\wedge\ Init$
  $\wedge\ \Box[Down \vee Up]_a$
  $\wedge\ \text{WF}_a(Down)$
  $\wedge\ \text{WF}_a(Up)$

Running the spec against the model checker passes again. What if we want to verify the elevator eventually always goes to the top, not just to 2F. Let's modify the Liveness property again:

$Liveness \triangleq$
  $\wedge\ a = BOTTOM \rightsquigarrow a = TOP$

The model checker now reports the following violation:

Error: Temporal properties were violated.
Error: The following behavior constitutes a counter-example:

```
State 1: <Initial predicate>
a = 1
State 2: <Up line 10, col 5 to line 11, col 17 of
  module elevator>
a = 2
Back to state 1: <Down line 13, col 5 to line 14,
  col 17 of module elevator>
```

The model checker identified a case where the elevator is perpetually stuck going between 1F and 2F but never goes to 3F. Weak fairness is no longer enough, because the the elevator is not stuck on 2F repeatedly, but stuck going *between* 1F and 2F. This is where we need strong fairness.

15.3   Strong Fairness

Strong fairness is defined as:

$$\Box\Diamond(ENABLED\langle A\rangle_v) \Rightarrow \Box\Diamond\langle A\rangle_v \qquad (15.2)$$

The difference between weak and strong fairness is the *eventually always* vs. *always eventually*.

In weak fairness, once the state machine is stuck in a state forever, the state machine always transitions to a possible next state permitted by the *Spec* (eg. if the elevator is stuck on 1F but can go to 2F, it will). With strong fairness, the elevator doesn't need to be stuck on 2F to go to 3F. If the elevator *always eventually* makes it to 2F, it *always eventually* go to 3F.

Intuitively we are tempted to enable strong fairness like so:

$Spec \triangleq$
  $\wedge\ Init$
  $\wedge\ \Box[Up \vee Down]_a$
  $\wedge\ \mathrm{WF}_a(Down)$
  $\wedge\ \mathrm{SF}_a(UP)$

However, model checker *still* reports the same violation.

If we take a closer look at the enabling condition for *Up*, it only requires a current floor to be not the *top floor*. When the elevator is stuck in a loop going Up and Down between 1F and 2F indefinitely, strong fairness for Up is *already satisfied*. What we want is strong fairness on *Up* for *every floor*, instead of *any floor except top floor*. So if the elevator makes it to 2F once, it will *always eventaully* go to 3F. If the elevator makes it to 3F once, it will *always eventaully* go to 4F, and so on. The following is the change required:

$Spec \triangleq$
  $\wedge\ Init$
  $\wedge\ \Box[Up \vee Down]_a$
  $\wedge\ \mathrm{WF}_a(Down)$
  $\wedge\ \forall f \in BOTTOM \mathinner{\ldotp\ldotp} TOP - 1:$
    $\wedge\ \mathrm{WF}_a(Up \wedge f = a)$

With this change, the model checker will pass.

Chapter 16

Liveness

While safety properties can catch per-state contradictions, liveness properties allow you to verify the behavior across a series of states. This is TLA+'s *superpower*. Designers are rarely interested only in the correctness of individual states in the system, but also the correctness of system *across* a set of states.

This book has provided a few examples of liveness properties so far: eg. The elevator eventually makes it to the top floor, consensus protocol eventually converges, the scheduling algorithm guarantees a lock requester eventually gets the lock, etc. I argue any system worth the reader's time to model using TLA+ must have interesting liveness properties to verify.

Unfortunately, liveness check also takes *much* longer, since the very definition of verifying property across a series of states makes the task very hard to parallelize. Care must go into refining the model to keep the model checker runtime reasonable. In this chapter, we will discuss a simple state machine example to illustrates liveness properties.

Assume a simple three-system system:

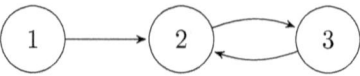

This can be described by the following spec:

─────────────────── MODULE *liveness* ───────────────────

EXTENDS *Naturals*
VARIABLES *counter*
$vars \triangleq \langle counter \rangle$

$EventuallyAlways \triangleq \Diamond \Box (counter = 3)$
$AlwaysEventually \triangleq \Box \Diamond (counter = 3)$

$Init \triangleq$
$\quad \wedge counter = 0$

$Inc \triangleq$
$\wedge counter' = counter + 1$

$Dec \triangleq$
$\wedge counter' = counter - 1$

$Next \triangleq$
$\quad \vee \wedge counter \neq 3$
$\qquad \wedge Inc$
$\quad \vee \wedge counter = 3$
$\qquad \wedge Dec$

$Spec \triangleq$
$\quad \wedge Init$
$\quad \wedge \Box [Next]_{vars}$
$\quad \wedge \mathrm{WF}_{vars}(Next)$

───

Note the fairness description in the spec. Without fairness the spec is allowed to stutter and fail any liveness property checks.

16.1 Always Eventually

We want to verify the system *always eventually* transition state 3. This can be described by the following liveness property:

$$AlwaysEventually \triangleq \Box\Diamond(counter = 3)$$

Once the system makes it to state 3, the system is stuck in a loop transitioning states 2 and 3. It doesn't *remain* in state 3, but it does *always eventually* transition to state 3. The system as described fulfills this liveness property.

16.2 Eventually Always

However, the system does not *eventually always* remain in state 3, because the system toggles between state 2 and 3. The liveness property to check the system *eventually always* transition to and remain state 3 is shown below:

$$EventuallyAlways \triangleq \Diamond\Box(counter = 3)$$

To satisfy this liveness property, we will need to *remove* the the transition from 3 to 2, which updates the state diagram like below:

We need to remove the corresponding *Dec* action from Next:

$Next \triangleq$
  $\wedge\ counter \neq 3$
  $\wedge\ Inc$

The system now *eventually always* remains in state 3, satisfying the liveness property.

Note that the system still *always eventually* makes it to state 3, so the updated spec satisfies both *AlwaysEventually* and *EventuallyAlways* liveness properties. This is not to say the designer should always use *eventually always*. Some system may *never* converge onto a fixed state. For example, in a consensus system, any given server may crash and disturb the converged state. In such case *eventually always* will never be true, but *always eventually* can be true.

16.3   Leads To

Leads to provides a *cause-and-effect* description. In this example, we can describe state 0 *leads to* state 3:

state 0 leads to state 3: TRUE
$$LeadsTo \triangleq counter = 0 \rightsquigarrow counter = 3$$

state 0 leads to state 4: FALSE - model checker reports a violation
$$LeadsTo \triangleq counter = 0 \rightsquigarrow counter = 4$$

Note that *leads to* is only evaluated if the left-hand side is *true*. If the right-hand side is updated to counter = 4, the liveness the property will fail as expected. However, if the left-hand side is false, then the liveness property is not evaluated since there isn't a state that satisfies the cause condition. For example, the model checker will not report violations for the following liveness property:

model checker will NOT report violation because cause condition never occur
$$LeadsTo \triangleq counter = 4 \rightsquigarrow counter = 3$$

Chapter 17

General Guideline

17.1 Be Skeptical

Even if model checker reports no violation, it is often worthwhile to dump and audit the states to make sure the specification is defined correctly.

```
tlc elevator -dump out > /dev/null && cat out.dump | head -n5
State 1:
a = 1
State 2:
a = 2
```

Designer can grep the output to look for the state being set to expected value to confirm the specification is working as intended.

17.2 Debug

Designer can insert prints or asserts with *PrintT* and *Assert* respectively, these may help root causing a bug when model checker reports fails.

An *Assert* dumps the backtrace leading up to it, but does not include values of any non-state variables. For example, if the state

145

includes with local macros using *LET..IN* semantics or *RECURSIVE* function calls, the associated values will not be displayed. Prints do not help in this case either. Since the model checker explores the states using BFS, the print order is not guaranteed.

To display any intermediary values, designer can add an auxiliary debug variable to the system definition. The debug variable will be dumped as part of the state backtrace.

17.3   Dead Lock

Deadlock typically happens when the model checker runs out of things to do. This can be a result of an incomplete specification definition, where certain edge cases were not accounted for. The model checker typically provides a fairly comprehensive backtrace leading up to the deadlock to simplify debugging.

17.4   Safety Properties

Designer should add as many system safety properties as possible to catch problems early. Safety properties are checked at the end of every state and impose very little overhead to overall execution.

17.5   Live Lock

Livelock happens when the model checker identifies a case where the system is oscillating between states without making progress towards the final goal. An example is the elevator stuck going between two floors instead of going to the top floor, or the system is stuck dropping and retransmitting the same packet.

These can be fixed by providing additional fairness descriptions to the specification, instructing the model checker how to prioritize transitions to take.

For a detailed fairness description please refer to Chapter 15.

17.6   Liveness Properties

While verifying liveness properties is super useful, the model checker at the time of writing can only verify liveness properties sequentially. To verify liveness, model checker must first identify the strongly connected component in the graph, and the algorithm currently implemented does not support parallelization.

The general recommendation is to only define and verify liveness properties if the specification is sufficiently small.

17.7   Fully Verification

Fully verified a model provide extremely high confidence the specification is correct. However, since the specification complexity grows exponentially, designer may need to get creative to reduce the model to allow the model checker can run in a practical amount of time.

Since the model complexity grows exponentially, there's little value in attempting to hyper-optimize implementation detail. Designers should focus on simplifying the model by removing non-critical features and focus verifying features with the highest return on investment.

One way of trimming out the low-value part of a specification is to audit the state dump. Even in the case of a non-terminating run, a partial state dump may help identify low-value abstractions that can be removed from the spec.

One key value of TLA+ is it highlights all the corner cases in the system. Even if the designer ends up simplifying the specification, it still likely highlights certain conditions the designer was previously unaware of.

17.8 Simulation and Generation

While fully verifying a specification is always ideal, it is not always practical. With sufficient complexity, the model checker will not be able to verify the specification in reasonable time. That said, it is still worthwhile to verify the specification by running the model checker in either simulation or generation mode. Simulation is the legacy simulation mode where the model checker keeps running without termination. Generation mode also causes the model checker to run without termination, but applies uniform probability distribution on selecting next state transition.

Even for a complex specification, the majority of violation will be caught very quickly per 80/20 rule. For some problem domain this may be good enough, and is certainly better than no verification at all.

Chapter 18

Data Structure

TLA+ fundamentally supports two different data structures: *Set* and *Function*. All other data structures are built on-top of these two primitives.

18.1 Set

Set is an unordered set where every element in the set is unique. TLA+ Set includes common set operation including union, intersection, membership check, and more. Set is declared using the squiggly operator, {}.

The following defines a few Set usage examples:

$a \triangleq \{0, 1, 2\}$
$b \triangleq \{2, 3, 4\}$

$\{0, 1, 2, 3, 4\}$
$c \triangleq a \cup b$

$\{2\}$
$d \triangleq a \cap b$

$\{0, 1, 3, 4\}$ - c substracts d

$$k \triangleq c \setminus d$$

18.2   Function

Function is similar to unordered map in other data structures, supporting key value association and lookup. Functions are defined using square brackets, $[]$.

The following provides a few examples of function:

$$SetA \triangleq \{\,\text{"a"},\ \text{"b"},\ \text{"c"}\,\}$$
$$SetB \triangleq \{\,\text{"c"},\ \text{"d"},\ \text{"e"}\,\}$$

Create a mapping with keys a, b, c with values 0, 0, 0
$$a \triangleq [k \in SetA \mapsto 0]$$
$$b \triangleq [k \in SetB \mapsto 1]$$

Concatenate
$$c \triangleq a @@ b$$

Subtraction
$$d \triangleq [x \in (\text{DOMAIN } c \setminus \text{DOMAIN } b) \mapsto c[x]]$$

Create a mapping with keys a, b, c with values {}, {}, {}
$$e \triangleq [k \in SetA \mapsto \{\}]$$

Create a mapping that is the same as e, except key a's value is "a", "b", "c"
$$f \triangleq [e \text{ EXCEPT } ![\text{"a"}] = \{\,\text{"a"},\ \text{"b"},\ \text{"c"}\,\}]$$

18.3   Tuple

A tuple is an ordered queue, which is implemented using *function* with ordered keys starting at 1. For example, a tuple of a, b, c is actually an unordered map of keys 1, 2, 3 mapping to a, b, c. A tuple is represented using double angle brackets.

$$a \triangleq \langle 0,\ 1,\ 2 \rangle$$
$$b \triangleq \langle 2,\ 3,\ 4 \rangle$$

tuple: 0, 1, 2, 2, 3, 4
$$c \triangleq A \circ B$$

tuple: 0, 1, 2, 3
$$c2 \triangleq Append(A, 3)$$

gets head: 0
$$c3 \triangleq Head(A)$$

removes head: 1, 2
$$c4 \triangleq Tail(A)$$

6
$$d \triangleq Len(c)$$

TRUE - every c[x] is not 10

First tuple element is at index 1 (not 0)
$$e \triangleq \forall\, x \in 1 \, .. \, Len(c) : c[x] \neq 10$$

TRUE - there exists a c[x] that is 2
$$f \triangleq \exists\, x \in 1 \, .. \, Len(c) : c[x] = 2$$

{3, 4} - when index is 3 or 4, c[x] = 2
$$g \triangleq \{x \in 1 \, .. \, Len(c) : c[x] = 2\}$$

18.4   Patterns

18.4.1   Set Comprehension

We can also construct a set from an existing set by defining filtering criteria:

{0, 1, 2} - all elements less than 3
$$i \triangleq \{x \in c : x < 3\}$$

18.4.2   Set and Function Size

We can check the size of a set using *Cardinality* function:

$Cardinality(set)$

Note keys of a function can be extracted as a set by applying the *DOMAIN* operator. The following is a way to determine the function size:

Cardinality(DOMAIN *function*)

18.4.3   Conditonal

We can use define conditionals with Set:

TRUE - because 4 in c is bigger than 3
$$e \triangleq \exists\, x \in c : x > 3$$

FALSE - nothing in c is bigger than 5
$$f \triangleq \exists\, x \in c : x > 5$$

FALSE - not all elements in c are smaller than 3
$$g \triangleq \forall\, x \in c : x < 3$$

TRUE - all elements in c are smaller than 3
$$h \triangleq \forall\, x \in c : x < 5$$

18.4.4   Loop with Recursion

Iterating through a set of values sequentially can be modeled using recursion:

RECURSIVE *FindNextToken*(_, _)
FindNextToken(*key*, *ring*) $\triangleq$
    LET
        condition(*v*) $\triangleq$
            (*ring*[*v*]["state"] = *StateOnline*
            $\lor$ *ring*[*v*]["state"] = *StateLeaving*)
               $\land$ *ring*[*v*]["token"] = *key*
        exists $\triangleq$ $\exists\, v \in$ DOMAIN *ring* : *condition*(*v*)
        owner $\triangleq$ CHOOSE *only* $\in$ DOMAIN *ring* : *condition*(*only*)
    IN
        IF *exists* THEN
          owner

ELSE
$$FindNextToken((key + 1)\%N, \ ring)$$
Make sure the recursion termination condition is defined correctly, otherwise model checker will report memory related runtime error.

18.4.5   Variable Update

Updating a variable on state transition boundary is often done using *EXCEPT* keyword:

$$f \triangleq [e \text{ EXCEPT } ![\text{"a"}] = \{\text{"a"}, \text{"b"}, \text{"c"}\}]$$

The limitation with the *EXCEPT* keyword is it permits update of a single key. This can be solved more generically by iterating through a set:

$$local\_ring = [i \in RGs \mapsto$$
$$[j \in RGs \mapsto$$
$$\text{IF } i = SeedRG \land j = SeedRG$$
$$\text{THEN } seed$$
$$\text{ELSE } \textit{offline}]]$$

We can apply the same trick when working with functions by using the *DOMAIN* keyword and iterate through the keys as a set:

$$kv' = [x \in \text{DOMAIN } kv \cup \{key\} \mapsto \text{IF } x = key \text{ THEN } value \text{ ELSE } kv[x]]$$

Chapter 19

Reference

Bibliography

[1] Specifying Systems, https://lamport.azurewebsites.net/tla/book.html

[2] Verifying Hyperproperties with TLA, https://lamport.azurewebsites.net/pubs/hyper2.pdf

[3] TLA Toolbox, https://github.com/tlaplus/tlaplus

[4] TLA+ Community Modules, https://github.com/tlaplus/CommunityModules

[5] Fairness in TLA+, https://sriku.org/posts/fairness-in-tlaplus/

[6] Backblaze Durability Calculates at 99.999999999% — And Why It Doesn't Matter, https://www.backblaze.com/blog/cloud-storage-durability/

[7] In Search of an Understandable Consensus Algorithm, https://raft.github.io/raft.pdf

[8] raft.tla, https://github.com/ongardie/raft.tla

[9] Wrangling monotonic systems in TLA+, https://ahelwer.ca/post/2023-11-01-tla-finite-monotonic/

[10] C10k problem, https://en.wikipedia.org/wiki/C10k_problem

[11] Dining Philosophers, https://en.wikipedia.org/wiki/Dining_philosophers_problem

[12] A GPU Algorithm for Detecting Strongly Connected Components, https://userweb.cs.txstate.edu/ mb92/papers/sc23c.pdf

[13] Keynote Fifteen years of formal methods at AWS, https://www.youtube.com/watch?v=HxP4wi4DhA0

[14] How Amazon Web Services Uses Formal Methods, https://cacm.acm.org/research/how-amazon-web-services-uses-formal-methods/